Karis Lee

# WRITE OUTSIDE THE LINES
## a creativity catapult

## By Cathy Altman Nocquet

To my parents and brother,
for making me this way...

and to my husband and daughter,
for putting up with it.

**A NOTE TO PARENTS ....**

In this age of instant information, our children are bombarded by screens flashing facts, opinions and graphics. Their ability to process this input and form original, interesting ideas will be their added value in life. For this, they'll need to think laterally, "outside the box."

Too many schools fall short when it comes to creative development. This is what inspired the writing workshops which led to this book. In it are many exercises children can do in any order, with or without their parents. They can think about their responses before they write, or attack the blank page cold, letting out whatever comes to mind. Both approaches help develop creative thinking.

Regular or occasional creative "workouts" with this book will get kids to reconsider before declaring they "have no ideas" and can keep them from saying "I'm bored." This has been the case with hundreds of students since the workshops began in 2008.

Kids won't always like what they produce, but that's part of the experience. They're free to try something different the next time they write. Soon, they'll trust themselves to be able to respond to the prompts in a way they'll find satisfying, in their own style and with their own "voice". Children who have trouble writing down their ideas can speak into a recorder or dictate to a willing typist. Yes, even 8 year-olds have their own creative styles. You'll see.

You may wish to start **a writing group** in your home, in which kids work on separate assignments while sitting around the table, attack the group workouts in this book, or even take turns making up assignments. Do this and your home will quickly become the popular place to be after school. If the kids are at the age where they don't want you sitting in, they'll still be thrilled to show you how clever and imaginative they can be.

## ... AND OTHER EX-KIDS

You don't have to be a kid to find a creative outlet in these exercises. Groups in the writing workshop now include college students and adults older than their parents.

So many people grow up believing they're "not at all creative". This is biologically impossible. Our brains are wired for intuitive responses; you just have to note yours, and you'll see you can write, as well. You've evolved into an adult, now let your creativity catch up.

If the first exercises feel too basic, go to the more difficult ones. Each assignment can be answered artfully, however. There's a challenging creative workout possible at any age.

**FOREWORD**

**... Then SIDEWAYS, to your creative adventure!**

Do you like writing? If you answer "yes", then this book is for you. If you answer "no", then this book is even more for you. It presents creative writing in a fun, original way. Just turn to any page and try an assignment. You can work on them in any sequence.

When you think creatively, you'll see that every idea can be a good one. Just set your brain loose. Can you imagine a brain running free? Draw or describe it, now. Does it run with 2 legs, or 83 or with one hand turning a wheel? Does your brain have a face or wear a hat? Is it reading a manual on astrophysics?

Don't worry if you have trouble drawing what you describe in words, or can't quite find the words to fit your drawing. While you use this book, you'll get better at all creative work, even if you can only trace your hand to make a Thanksgiving turkey. But do try everything. When it comes to creativity, there are no wrong answers.

Chances are you've already begun "working" and this is only the Foreword. The exercises that follow will help you create original characters, settings and plots. You can use your own writing notebook, to keep your work together. Don't worry about "ruining" it by writing and drawing in the margins; just think of it as your "work in progress", the way professional writers do. Ready to join the ranks of the creative? Then, give a creative rally cry:

Kowabunga! Geronimo! Pen, do your stuff! Gitchee gitchee! Wahooo!

What's your creative cry?

**TABLE OF CONTENTS**

**Chapter 7: Cherish Your Garden Worms** *(p.121)*

More original prompts, inspired by sounds, art, and foreign languages. Taste revenge and travel in time. Learn to keep the best parts as you edit. Never stop taking notes for new stories, poems and dreams.

**Epilogue: "Section Snake: Return of the Bad Seed"** *(p.145)*

What happens with Nardo? Send in your ending to the story and the best one, with your permission, will appear in the next book.

# CHAPTER 1:

## MEET YOUR MIND, A FERTILE FACTORY

"What do you need to write a story?" Cathy asked the first group of workshop students.

"A pen!" "Paper!" the replies shot out.

"What else?"

Silence.

Then, "An idea!"

"Good. There are times when the idea you start with turns into something else, but that's part of the fun. What more do you need?"

"A character!"

"How many?"

"Two!" "More than two!"

"Can you have a story with just one character?"

Opinion was divided, but they were now all engaged in the debate.

"We'll try writing some, and see. How about a story with no characters?"

"That's impossible!"

"Let's suppose it is possible and see what happens."

Thinking creatively allows you to assume anything is possible, then give it a try. If you're like most kids, you love experiments, and once you're inspired, you'll love writing, too. At school, you might have to worry about spelling, grammar, and skipping lines between paragraphs, but for the exercises that follow, you're allowed to turn your notebooks sideways and write in waves with different sized letters, if you'd like. Jot whatever comes to mind in the margins, as long as you can read what you wrote, and apply your creativity while completing the assignment. (Sometimes the best ideas are the ones found outside the lines. Cathy's so sure of that, she turned it into the title!)

Many students assume there must be "rules". But when they ask "Are we supposed to…? Or "Is it okay if we….?" the answer in the workshop is "Any way you like is fine." Having too many guidelines could train you to churn out stories that seem "manufactured". The writing workshop is about inventing new ways out of as many creative messes as you can conjure up. Once you learn how to come up with fresh ideas, you can organize them to make great stories.

**Pen, Paper and Your Brain**

So, what DO you need to write a story?" The **rational** part of brain would list practical things like paper and pencil, if it could talk. (*Hey, what if it could? Write that down on* **your "IDEAS" page**. *You'll learn to keep an IDEAS page in the next section*). The **intuitive** part of your brain supplies the ideas and characters for your story. One part organizes and orders, the other part dreams and creates.

Some people have a stronger rational side, and some have a stronger intuitive one, but everyone has both. Even that weird guy at the video store who drools and mumbles to himself. So which side of your brain do you need when you write? Both.

Without organization, your creative impulses may not make sense to other people. And without your intuitive part, your stories might seem as uninspired as dishwater. (*Wait! What if dishwater were inspiring? These are the kinds of question experimenting creative writers need to ask themselves every day.*)

Which of the following is rational and which is creative? Pondering, spontaneity, list making, having a hunch, making a random choice, making a careful choice, day dreaming, evaluating, acting on impulse, inventing, editing, indulging whimsy, analyzing. You'll do all of this as you make your way through this book.

Remember, YOUR MIND IS A FERTILE FACTORY, active even when you think it's idle.

**DRAW YOUR FERTILE FACTORY**. Does it seem to be in a hollow tree, in a sea shell, or in a sports arena? Is there an oven, a conveyor belt or a potter's wheel? You decide.

*(Work in your notebook)*

**NOTE**: Most of you will find your own order to do the exercises in this book. If you write the **date** on each one, you'll see how your work changes with experience. You can also describe how you feel that day. Ready to hop in a marathon? Mad enough to stick out your tongue at a koala bear? Some days might just be inside out, rainy outside, but sunny in your chest. Write about anything that strikes you.

Are you resisting? (Which part of your brain leads you to resist?) Then, imagine what an empty mind would look like.

**DESCRIBE OR DRAW A MIND WITH NO IDEAS**. Is it an empty box? A desert with tumbleweeds rolling by? A dusty drawer? An airless chunk in outer space? Aha. You can visualize something already, can't you? That means you have ideas.

Cathy's philosophy is that you need not hunt for ideas; instead, you can **let your ideas find you**. Ideas might float by like snowflakes or spring from the earth like weeds. Just reach out and grab one. If you don't like that one, let another one tickle the soles of your feet or settle on the tip of your nose.

**DRAW A BUNCH OF IDEAS**. Are they in a "sea" or joined by "roots"? What colors and shapes are they? How do they move? Do they have feelings? What if they did?

*(Work in your notebook)*

**DESCRIBE "AN IDEA'S DAY"** Does your idea have a name? How about Goober, Barbareena or Doorknob the Terrible?

*(Work in your notebook)*

**CATHY'S CREATIVE CREDO**

Please place one hand on your **heart** and the other on your **brain**, then pledge.

**"I promise, to use my brain creatively, and to do the assignments wholeheartedly, staying open to all ideas, no matter what."**

Now, make faces and do a joyful dance. You're a member of the team.

**COPY THE CREDO ONTO A SEPARATE PAPER, THEN ILLUSTRATE IT.** You can hang it on the wall of your room, to remind you of your commitment to creativity.

**YOUR NOTEBOOK PARTNER**

Students each bring a notebook to the workshop, used only for creative writing. In the first class, they're asked to turn to the last page of their notebooks. This throws them off. Why start at the back?

"Write **'IDEAS'**. When you think of a good set up for a story, or a line for a poem, or anything else that sparks you creatively, write it down. This way, whether you end up using it or not, you won't forget it ."

The rational students usually ask: "But it's the last page. What happens when we run out of room?"

Start working on writing exercises from the front, while you fill up the notebook with ideas from the back. When you get to the middle, it's time to buy a new notebook.

The idea of "working backwards" seems fun to some of the kids. But others wonder where they've landed. Taravina, among other magical places. You'll go there, too, in a few more chapters.

Try not to use your notebook for daily reminders such as

*"Remember Dentist 5pm"* unless you do something with them:
*"Antonetta was 11 minutes late for her dentist appointment,
sweating as she ran down the rainy street. She noticed she was as
soaked on the inside as she was on the outside. That was an
interesting concept, but it felt gross. Now, she could forget about
getting her homework done in the waiting room; she'd be
escorted straight to the examining room, with a sneer from the
receptionist. But just as she reached for the office door, an
enormous blue hand plunged down from the clouds and scooped
her up, high above the dripping tree branches ....."*

**Finish and illustrate this story in your notebook.**

Even with a notebook that's just for your creative writing, you
may end up taking notes on other scraps of paper. At least, that's
what many writers and artists do. As soon as you can, transfer
them to your **"notebook partner"** so they're all together. The
more good ideas you note, the more you'll have to write about,
and the more you'll end up writing.

## SPEAKING OF "PARTNERS", MEET NARDO

Everyone has a disparaging voice inside, whether playing chess,
painting a portrait or practicing for the High Jump. "You can't do
it", "Who do you think you're kidding?" "Don't make a fool of

yourself." Why not give a body to that voice and then make friends with the creature trying to block your work?

Cathy's creature is called Nardo and he lives in her guts. Nardo is a sneaky, snaky character, and not very scary; he's more like a puppet you'd make from an old sock. Nardo might have one button eye and one embroidered eye and think this gives him a cool, "pirate look." Cathy would let him believe it.

Nardo can still undermine her, though, giving her that feeling of "butterflies" in her stomach, when she's nervous. He reminds her of her inadequate knowledge of history or comments about her caustic wit that not everyone finds appealing. Nardo even teases her about her haircut. Cathy knows Nardo will continue to exist no matter what she does, so she decided to develop him into a character.

*"It's about time I had a platform to express myself," Nardo sneers, stretching his body tall, so his one good eye looks straight into Cathy's.*

*"And who made that possible?" Cathy asks.*

*"I did!" Nardo says.*

*A staring contest ensues. Nardo blinks.*

*"Go to sleep, Nardo." Cathy says. Today, she's the mature one.*

*Nardo yawns, coils his long, reptilian body and rests his head on top, like a pillow.*

Your censoring creature need not be an animal. It could be a carnivorous plant, a parasitic insect, tyrannical teacher, a miniature militant or a talking pebble. Giving a body to the voice inside you makes it a fairer fight. Decide where your creature "lives" and what might happen between you one day--- not just your dialogue, but actions. Does he/she use your credit card and order a dozen pizzas?

Does he dial "time" in Japan, then leave the phone connected to run up your bill?

**DESCRIBE AND DRAW YOUR CREATURE**, the one who tries to discourage you.

It can be very satisfying to let your creature get the upper hand in a story and win a battle against you, because, having written the story, you claim the real victory! **PUT YOUR CREATURE IN A STORY (You can use this character in more stories, later).**

As you work in, around and through this book, you may come up with good ideas for writing exercises yourself. Be sure to explore those, too.

*"No, don't. Just send all your ideas to 'Nardo, Editor in Chief'. They were probably things I thought of before you were born, so I'll take the credit."*

*"Don't worry. He will not."*

*"Watch me."*

*"Nardo, go to sleep."*

*Is this a fair match? Cathy's 5'4" in heels, and he's 14' of winding worm! More about Nardo later. He and his writer host go way back.*

**TRUST YOUR FERTILE FACTORY**

Some teachers will tell you to keep every single thing you write, but Cathy prefers keeping only her favorite and latest drafts, figuring she can always come up with more words and ideas later. She'd rather not have to wade through a swamp of old writing if she can avoid it.

*Hey, imagine the writing you toss aside could fester into a* **swamp***! You've just dumped some poems you don't like into the murky water, and as you walk away, your foot gets caught in a "b." It's the "b" from the word "ambivalence" and the weight of all the letters pulls you under.*

*You can't breathe, you swallow some swamp water. Blech! Now, pull yourself out of the swamp and walk away from the writing you didn't want to keep. Saved! You're sure to get a fresh new idea with your next breath!*

After using this book for a while, you'll be able to count on your mind as a **FERTILE FACTORY,** and know you'll always get another idea you like later. So it's no big deal to throw pages away. Of course, some people like to look back at everything they've written, and if you think you'd like that better, you're absolutely welcome to work that way.

*Here's a thought: Some people feel safer with all their stuff. Maybe these are the same ones who still sleep surrounded with stuffed animals when they're 25 years old. Could that be a good idea for a character? Someone who even takes stuffed animals to work with him, and he's a surgeon or a carpenter, or a fortune teller.....*You take it from here, okay?

**WRITE ABOUT A CHARACTER THAT LIKES KEEPING EVERYTHING, THEN DRAW HIM OR HER.**

*(Work in your notebook)*

If you're not a "saver" and at the other extreme, you may cross out your ideas as fast as you note them, and never feel your beginnings are worth finishing. If that's the case, try not to judge your writing too quickly. Leave it, and see if there's anything you can do with it later. There usually is. If you reject every effort you make, you'll have nothing left to work with! Using this book will teach you how to **make even the most boring ideas interesting**, so don't lose hope!

## WRITE DOWN FIVE "BORING STORY " IDEAS. THIS TAKES SOME CREATIVITY, DOESN'T IT?

*(Work in your notebook)*

## MAKE BOREDOM FASCINATING

There are times you'll feel inert, like a sack of potatoes, and won't find the energy to do anything. You can still be creative, though. First, try to **locate your brain**. Is it standing in line at the airport, hoping to board a plane to Rio? It's possible it just wanted a break. Allow it. Find some other things your brain could be off doing without you.

*(Work in your notebook)*

Now **stare at the wall**. Are these tiny bumps in the paint, or a pattern on the wallpaper? Make a city in the texture or design and describe the inhabitants. Name the city. Is there a mayor?

## WRITE ABOUT A TOWN ON THE SURFACE OF THE WALL. DRAW THE HOUSES AND INHABITANTS.

*(Work in your notebook)*

If you're too bored to even stare at the wall, which is a very serious case of boredom, then think: "Where would I rather be?" Swimming? In a lake or a pool? With friends or alone? Is your dog watching you from the shore, and/or is an alligator swimming alongside you? Describe your bathing suit, if you're wearing onc. Maybe there's another swimmer there you don't know. Name that character...

*(Work in your notebook)*

You can also write a very **creative description** of your boredom. Does your empty mind remind you of a supermarket with nothing on the shelves? How does it feel being there? What can you see, hear, smell, touch and taste? Think of another original image for boredom, then write about it and draw it.

*(Work in your notebook)*

You're mind's not so empty now, is it? You've given dullness and monotony a whole new value!

There are plenty of short and fun exercises in these chapters to get you back on track when you feel discouraged.

*"Or, you can listen to me, Nardo: Just eat some caramels and lie down. Soon all your ideas will float away and you'll take a nice, long nap."*

*"Leave them alone, you sneaky snake. They're using this book because they have what it takes and are ready to write!"*

*Swarthy Nardo, slinking in his dark glasses, draws Cathy into his confidence again and again. How lovely the pink and yellow tulips were that arrived the day of the three quarter moon! How sweet the note that read "I wuv you!" But when she touched the flowers, they crumbled. Fakes, made of highly allergenic paper. She sneezed for a week.*

If he goes to so much trouble, Nardo must care about her on some level, right? *Right?* Maybe she should think of it this way: Nardo sometimes keeps her from writing but he sure gives her reason to write!

You may like working on a computer. It makes it easy to keep a file for each of your stories, and add or delete things as you go. Once you're happy with a change, you're allowed to erase the old version, if you'd like. Keeping eighteen drafts of a document would drive some writers nuts, but, if it makes you feel more comfortable, it's fine to work that way, too.

Do write down all the bits and pieces of ideas that seem interesting. **ANYTHING can be expressed creatively** and become a story or a poem.

Let thumbtacks, hyenas, dust motes, artichokes and droplets of perspiration inspire you. There's something right about even the worst drivel, we'll prove that later. So never despair. Remember your fertile factory. It's at work planning tonight's dreams even while you're focused on that freckled kid at recess, picking at the scab on her knee. You'll soon learn to keep the interesting part of your writing and add just what's missing to make it great. You can even add drawings as you go. Don't strive for "perfection", since there's no such thing. Any story can always be changed a little, and made more intriguing, better. Think of some classics. What would you rather see different in "Hansel and Gretel"? What if the house wasn't made of gingerbread but sorbet, so melted, and the witch was a retired used car dealer? They could all meet at a Limbo contest in Switzerland, or..... You take it from here.

*(Work in your notebook)*

## WHEN TO WRITE

You may notice that the times **you get your best ideas, you're doing something else**. It's often something mechanical, when you're not aware you're thinking. Taking a shower, walking to the store, pouring your cereal in the morning. This is true for everyone. What happens is the creative, intuitive side of your brain is free to "roam" when the rational side has you doing something mechanical. Cathy was unloading the dishwasher when she got the idea for basing characters in a story on silverware. Swim laps this summer, and you'll probably have enough ideas to write a novel before school starts next year!

All this is to say that you don't need to chase ideas. They'll come to you, once you get in the habit of writing them down. The more open you are to thinking in new ways about new things, **the more ideas you'll have**. You'll become an expert on which ones to pursue and which ones to set aside. And remember that anything you write will have made you a better writer, even if you think it's terrible when it's done. The people too afraid to try never become writers.

Here's another rule you can break: Don't force yourself to write when you're really not in the mood. That's the time to take a walk and let your brain go on holiday. But the more you do write when you feel happy about it, **the more often you'll want to write**. Forcing yourself to sit down and produce pages is like chasing ideas. Pretty fruitless. You'll soon trust that ideas will come to you more and more easily.

*"Ignore the above. It's completely wrong. Write everyday from 4:32 to 5:18pm. Cross out tons, crumple the paper, and throw it on the floor. Find a board game you'd rather be playing, then yank it off the shelf, spilling all the pieces. Then laugh."*

*"Nardo! That's unacceptable! It's not only negative, it's destructive. You're grounded, buster!"*

*"Can I at least give you a special hug, in honor of Armadillo Day?"*

*"All right, but don't squeeze too hard."*

TSK TSK...

**WHAT TO KEEP**

Anything that gets your attention. Assignments in this book you feel you did well. Good starts you didn't finish and other ideas you note, to work on later.

Some think that if you don't chronicle what it felt like to be a kid, there's no way you can remember it once you're an adult, but Cathy does. Vividly. If that means she never grew up, at least it's been entertaining.

The plastic **alphabet** set she had when she was 3 later gave her the idea that any letter could be any color. Amazing how many people agree that "A" is red. But try telling them that "P" is light blue or that "J" is orange. Since giving letters colors is absurd in the first place, it makes for an entertaining argument. It could even become a story!

Cathy didn't have a set of **numbers**, but she's since given each of the counting digits, one through nine, a color. Which colors would you give each number?

**GIVE NUMBERS AND LETTERS COLORS, AND EXPLAIN YOUR CHOICES**. Your explanations don't have to be logical. Colors are very emotional.

*(Work in your notebook)*

Any **memory** you have, at any time in your life is useful in your writing. If you think there are things you might forget, then by all means, keep a journal or just jot things down in your writing notebook. Or, if you think the increasing number of notebooks would weigh you down, don't try to capture everything; you will always have **new memories**, and can reconstruct any childhood memory that interests you, whether or not it's accurate! Draw on anything from the past or present, to use in your creative thinking throughout your life. You can even use your future. Just invent it!

## WRITE DOWN A FEW THINGS YOU REMEMBER FROM WHEN YOU WERE YOUNGER

*(Work in your notebook)*

## FIND YOUR STYLE

Some people write lean prose while others feel more natural using elaborate wording. The more your write, the sooner you'll find your style or **"voice."** In the meantime, let the voices of other writers inspire you, but when possible, try to invent your own phrases instead of relying on theirs. Eventually, you'll craft words as only you can.

Express yourself freely, then take a good look at what you have. Is each sentence clear? Does it build on the sentence before and **move your story forward**? The exercises in this book will have you move your story backwards, sideways or diagonally, but it still must progress and stay interesting. If not, no one's going to enjoy it, including you. If you're not sure whether you should include a "detour" in another direction, try writing with and without it, then decide which version works better.

*"Neither works. Throw them both out."*

*"Gee, Nardo, thanks for your support."*

Some scientists say the intestines are "the second brain." No wonder that's where Cathy feels Nardo so often! He'd love to take over! But, the more he discourages her, the more she fights against it. Having him around is actually a great way to keep her on track!

## CUT THE FAT, PAINLESSLY

When you've just written something honest that came from **deep inside**, you're extra vulnerable to criticism. It's too personal, so too soon for the assault of outside opinions, even your own. So lay your writing on the desk and let a day pass. Once it's no longer next to your heart, you can be much more **objective** about it. Your writing becomes something outside you to analyze, and arrows of criticism won't penetrate your chest.

**Editing** gives you a good feeling when you see your work improve with each revision. Start by getting an overview. Reread the whole story in one sitting and don't make any changes yet. Hold a pencil, and make light check marks by the places you think might be confusing, too long or unneeded. You'll rework those passages later.

Now reread it all again, and notice which parts are essential. These are the elements that move your story ahead. Leave one out, and the story stops making sense. List these **essential elements**, in order, on a separate page. This gives you a **skeleton** onto which you can add "flesh" where it's needed. All the non-essential parts of your story are the **"flesh."**

Start by taking the **best**, most interesting bits first. You'll soon see where your descriptions get too long, when they take you too far from your storyline and when they slow down the action. Once you think you've added enough flesh, read your story through again. It's better already, isn't it?

Each time you delete or change something major, step back and reread it all again. One analogy to make is that of **cutting your bangs**. After each snip, check the effect in the mirror, and decide what comes next. If you keep your face too close to the mirror and cut too much, when you pull away to take stock of your work, you may find it looks pretty weird and not what you wanted! If you're bald and can't relate to this example, here's another one:

Imagine working on an **oil painting**. Towards the end, you work carefully because each dab of paint might be the last one you need. An experienced artist knows when the painting is finished. More touches after this point will only make it worse. That's why you, an artist-in-training, should be attentive towards the end of your "painting" and stop after each new dab of paint, before you go too far. If you're not a painter, either, maybe you should try cutting hair!

Forget about endings, bangs and paints for a while, and consider **beginnings**. Does your story start right away, or do you spend a long time with descriptions and explanations setting it up? As you reread your draft, there may be a place where you feel "Lights, camera, action! This is where it gets good!" That may be the real beginning of your story. Most readers can figure out who and what a story's about with minimal information, so are ready for a story to take off pretty quickly.

You usually know by the end of the first page if you like a book or not. Notice what it is that grabs you, and make sure your story has something that compelling right away. It doesn't have to be in the action, it can be the originality of a character, the setting or the style. What if your narrator was a character with a foreign accent and the descriptions were written with his grammatical errors and spelled to sound just like his speech? Anything different can be interesting and save readers from getting tired of books that always start and end in a predictable way.

## START A WRITING GROUP

Working with others who like writing can be incredibly fun. What's more, you can get comments on your writing that really help, whether you all work on the same assignment, or on separate ones. There are group prompts in a later chapter.

**Listen carefully** to the person reading his or her work. Then, it's that writer's turn to listen, while anyone who has a suggestion makes it. Be tactful. Critiques always start with a positive remark. Even the most terrible writing has something that's right about it. Is the character original? Is the set-up clever? Is the description of the weather in the story well executed?

Practice being a good group participant and finding **something positive** to say, before making your constructive suggestion. "Have you thought about trying..." is more supportive than "I hated when ..."

Make sure your initial praise is about the writing, not the person. If you say *"Gee, Trudi, you look so good in lime green. It makes your braces look shinier. And I really like the way you wound those braids around your head. Too bad your story's so awful!"* it won't be much help.

**You're free** to use the ideas people have about your story, or discard them. That's entirely up to you. But acknowledge their attempts to help. And do consider their ideas. They may just have a point.

When you meet again, you can read your revisions, or **move on** to do new work. If each member of the group is considerate, everyone benefits. And you'll probably end up laughing a lot.

*"Nardo, wipe that smirk off your face. And quit trying to swallow people's erasers."*

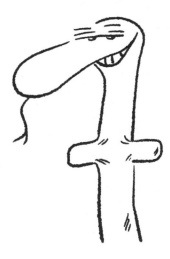

# CHAPTER 2:

# TILL YOUR BRAIN SOIL

In Chapter 1, you read about different ways to enable creativity: keeping an open mind, pursuing ideas in all directions (even the absurd!) and sharing work with others in a positive atmosphere. Now, you'll get into the specifics of the **Who** and **Where** of your stories:

## CHARACTERS AND SETTINGS

Can you have a story without characters? (It's better to try before you say "No"). What if you had an interesting setting in which things happened? A grassy field at dusk, and the sun sets. That would make for action you can describe, and the end of the story would be darkness with maybe the sound of a few crickets. It may not be the most riveting literature ever written, but it qualifies as a story in this workshop.

You can make **objects** into wonderful characters. Imagine a chair in a doctor's waiting room or a bench in a train station that is sat upon by dozens of people each day. Your character could be a soccer ball that keeps getting kicked, or one that's left behind when its owner goes to college. It could even be your writing notebook.

**Settings** also deserve your original thinking. Maybe a princess isn't locked in a castle, but in a bar of soap. Maybe Robin Hood gallivants in the sewer with a band of Merry Microbes. Not all stories about kids your age have to take place at school or at home when the alarm goes off, as mom calls "Honey, breakfast!"

The hero of your story can shoot pool in Wyoming, or camp with a Viking named Mason who thinks it's the 10th Century.

Start with the **strangest setting** you can find. What kind of story could take place inside an eyeball, in an ice cube tray or stuck to the bottom of a shoe?

Can you have a story that takes place **nowhere**? Would it float in space? Would it take place in a vacuum?

## WRITE A STORY THAT TAKES PLACE NOWHERE, AND ILLUSTRATE IT

*(Work in your notebook)*

**List some other strange settings on your "IDEAS" page at the back of your notebook.**

Now, find another **unusual location**, outside this time. It could be desert island where the natives aren't barefoot, but wear business suits, or a country where the language has no words, just stamping and clapping, or a zoo where animals wander loose and humans live in the cages.

## WRITE ONE SCENE THAT COULD HAPPEN IN THIS SETTING

*(Work in your notebook)*

Try placing a story in a **snow globe**, inside an ear, or in your pencil case. How completely can you describe this setting? What makes it a more interesting place for this particular story than a school or a park?

## WRITE YOUR STORY AND DRAW YOUR SETTING.

*(Work in your notebook)*

Your character wakes up inside a **cardboard box**. Where is he or she? What time of day is it and what is the weather? Is anyone else around?

*(Work in your notebook)*

Set a story in a **hallway** of any type. Where is it? Light or dark? Smooth or rough? Describe your characters and what happens to them.

*(Work in your notebook)*

Think up the strangest **jobs** you can, and put them in a story. If you don't feel ready to write a whole story, then list the jobs on your "IDEAS" page to use later. What would it be like to work as the quality control tester in a **button factory**, or to work in a **lighthouse**, make violin bows, or be a clown who entertains at hospitals?

*(Work in your notebook)*

Write a story in a world where everything is **broken**. The baseball bat is bent, the trampoline has holes. The roof is half off, the bathtub is cracked….Give this place a name. What kind of jobs do people have there? What is the national pastime?

*(Work in your notebook)*

Describe **Pet Heaven** in your own, original way. Suppose it's not all rainbows and unlimited dog biscuits? What could make this new world of animal spirits an interesting place? Are there automatic exercise mills with bouncing balls to chase? Is the floor made entirely of catnip-scented pillows? Give your heaven qualities you couldn't find on earth. Do clouds float ankle high all day? Is there harp music playing, or a mouse named Emma strumming a guitar? Write about and draw the Pet Heaven you imagine.

*(Work in your notebook)*

Your next story begins in a **hammock**, in a thick fog. Where are you and what happens? Is it tied up high, in the Amazonian forest, or on your neighbor's sheep farm, or is it right in your backyard?

Now, write a story that takes place in a **bowling alley.** Does this mean the characters have to bowl? Of course not. They can be trying on bowling shoes, using the rest room, standing by the drink machine or playing cards for most of the story.

*(Work in your notebook)*

A **Lost and Found** is a great place to set a story. Find one that interests you, decide what was lost or found by whom. Is it a bus station in Madrid, at a school in Ohio, at a five star resort in Hawaii?

*(Work in your notebook)*

Where in the world is **Taravina**? Don't bother trying to find it on a map, because it's nowhere to be seen. Invent this place and describe the landscape, inhabitants and customs. Some students put Taravina in Italy. One put it in his knapsack, one put it under the rubber band around her thick pony tail, and others put it outside our universe. How is life different in Taravina than where you live? More on Taravina in Music and Group Workout sections.

**MAKE A MAP OF TARAVINA** *in your notebook*

A setting in which a **simple action** occurs can trigger a whole story. Imagine a character **opening a gate with a key**. Where and what sort of gate is it? Wood? Iron? How large is the key? (This may reveal the age of the gate. Big keys used to open old gates). Now, think about where your character is going, through the gate, and why. What are some other simple actions that inspire you to write a story? Tying a shoe lace? Slamming a door? Shredding a document? Picking up something found on a beach? **List a few more simple actions, then write and illustrate your story.**

*(Work in your notebook)*

**Create a city** in a body part, armpit, ear, heart, lung. If it's in your mouth, are the teeth houses or people or neither? What is the role of the tongue? Try to make interesting choices instead of just writing obvious (and gross!) things that come to mind. This way, people will want to read it.

*(Work in your notebook)*

Set a story on a **window ledge**. What sort of characters might you use? A pigeon, who just landed there? A window cleaner, watching the people inside? A star gazer, impatient for nightfall? Someone gasping for breath, who opens the window for air?

*(Work in your notebook)*

Imagine a setting, and describe how and where it leads to a **secret place**. Try not to go through a wardrobe like the characters in Narnia. The secret place doesn't have to be magical, by the way; it may just be a private place to go think things over.

*(Work in your notebook)*

You should know by know that it's possible to set **an interesting story in an ordinary setting**, and write a conventional story in an interesting setting. Both can be well written, but you may as well try to make everything about your story unique.

*(Work in your notebook)*

*Nardo has managed to slither into Cathy's left sock and is making her foot itch. She tries to ignore him, but keeps hearing muffled laughter coming from her sneaker. But he's given her an idea: Write a story that takes place in a sock. Thanks, Nardo!*

*"GRRR! I mean, 'HISSSSS!!'"*

What a character! Now, it's your turn to generate some **characters** of your own. Think about how they **look and behave**. What are her or his dreams? Does he or she have a secret side no one knows? What stands out from his childhood? Where will she be in ten years?

Gather some **generic figurines** from your room; small toys that don't represent a famous character. You may have a duck, soldier, teen doll, fox and a kangaroo. It doesn't matter. Give each one the most obvious name and personality you can, based on how they look. For example, the blond figurine in the flowing pink dress holding a wand would be a fairy princess, not an apprentice plumber, and her name might be Tara Twinkle, not Brutus Von Bruiser.

Now, write a name and description of each character that are totally **unexpected**. Eventually, you can put two or more of these original characters in a scene together.

*(Work in your notebook)*

Cathy once had a coloring book with a character that stayed in her mind for decades. It was a **pig on roller skates**, wearing a striped t-shirt. How did a pig get a pair of roller skates, or a t-shirt? Did life get easier, harder, more fun, stranger once he had skates? Give an animal some sort of gadget and write about what happens.

**WRITE ABOUT YOUR CHARACTER** *in your notebook*

What kind of character does the name Bobo Bonehead, Wanda Wondrous, Trixie Slick, Ichabod Thickpitchet or **Hoopla Lollipooch** suggest? Now do this exercise again and make the descriptions even more original. If Ichabod was skinny, tall and bad at math the first time, now make him plump, short and a fast reader.

**DRAW YOUR CHARACTER** *in your notebook*

Imagine a man who is 75, tan and muscular with dyed blond hair, a fluorescent bathing suit and mirrored sunglasses. What would be a good, **surprising name** for him? Tiff Borax? Sir Regimar Huffinsterch? Would he be a lifeguard in North Carolina, a cashier in a donut shop in Omaha, an archaeologist, or something else?

**DESCRIBE YOUR CHARACTER** *in your notebook*

Make up more **distinctive looking characters** and give them unexpected names. Once you have that, you can add another dimension and **create a secret side** to the character. Might Tiff/Regimar also be a cartographer? Might he burst into tears whenever he hears someone sing "Happy Birthday"? Was he once in training for the Olympics as a figure skater?

*(Work in your notebook)*

Write a story including a character that does something **backwards.** Maybe he wears his shirt backwards, or answers his phone with a hearty "Goodbye?" Why? Do other people find that interesting or annoying?

*(Work in your notebook)*

Write a story about a boy with a **magnetic butt**. Imagine him trying to set the table, or walk through a jewelry store. Was he born that way, or was it the result of an accident? Do his relatives have similarly weird body parts, or is he alone?

*(Work in your notebook)*

Invent a character that's **half animal and half object**. Is it useful? Wild? Funny? Sad? How did it come to exist? Who else lives in its world?

*(Work in your notebook)*

Now, create characters from what you'd find in a **silverware** drawer. How does the personality of a spoon differ from that of a fork? Make up their voices. Now change their voices to make them more surprising. What about the spatula, carrot peeler and ice cream scoop? What are their dreams? How do they conflict? Write a scene with your characters and place it anywhere – In a nightclub in Tulsa, on safari in Kenya, hitchhiking across

Holland...

*(Work in your notebook)*

Create characters like none you've ever encountered: A cheetah deep sea diver, a princess who gets all her clothes in resale shops, **a talking boomerang**. List a few more to use later on your IDEAS page.

*(Work in your notebook)*

Invent the **secret side** of someone you know or someone you've seen. (You can choose someone to observe, then make up his hidden side) Is your local librarian really a body builder, devoted to her orchids? Is the guy at the dry cleaners a star of radio in Poland, a professional ballroom dancer, or both?...

*(Work in your notebook)*

You might need a mirror for this. Temporarily change something about your face or hair, so you look like someone else. Make your mouth tiny, puff up your cheeks, make one eyebrow go up and one go down...Name and describe this character, **your new alter ego.** Attribute qualities you wouldn't expect. Cathy gave herself ridiculous pigtails, called the character Pergoona, and made her a rocket scientist.

***"You flatter yourself."***

## PASTE A PHOTO OF YOUR ALTER EGO IN YOUR NOTEBOOK

Invent characters based on **playing cards**. Don't limit yourself to the face cards (Jack, Queen and King). Think how the personality of the four of clubs might differ from that of the eight of diamonds?

*(Work in your notebook)*

Invent an **upside down character.** This is a character either regularly or occasionally upside down compared to the rest of the world. Avoid bats and sloths, unless you do something very original with them.

*"I'd avoid them anyway!"*

*"Fraidy cat."*

*(Work in your notebook)*

Write and illustrate a story in which the characters are items in a **medicine cabinet.** How is the antacid different from the Band-Aids or the hairspray? Try to avoid making their personalities too close to what they do for people. For example, what if the moisturizer wasn't soothing? Remember, your story need not take place inside the medicine cabinet.

*(Work in your notebook)*

Put a small piece of paper on the table, next to a bread crumb: Presenting **Scrapetina and Crumbelina.** Imagine their biographies then put them in a story together.

*(Work in your notebook)*

Make any acceptable **gesture**, then invent a character that frequently uses that gesture. Male or female? Old or young? Fat or thin? Write a biography and speculate about the character's future.

*(Work in your notebook)*

Create a character that **expresses himself strangely**, either via gestures or the way he speaks, and have him describe how to tie a shoe or make breakfast. It could be someone who mixes the order of words when he speaks (one mixes he when order words the who speaks), or he could gesticulate wildly or unclearly. Make up whatever seems interesting, as long as readers can understand the directions he gives.

**DRAW YOUR CHARACTER, or make a collage about his favorite place to be.** *(Work in your notebook)*

Suppose there were characters called Bertha Thunderboom, Tyneesha Minicrumb and Professor Grexorious Pikwinkler. Write portraits of each of them, trying to make them **unlike** what their names suggest.

**DRAW YOUR CHARACTER** *in your notebook*

Choose **three adjectives** to describe yourself when you were four years old, three more to describe yourself when you were seven, and three more to describe yourself now. It doesn't matter if you had "happy, silly, babyish" one time and "shy, bookish, fearful" the next. There are no right or wrong answers. Now, invent a new character based one of the sets of adjectives. The character can be like you, or not at all! This is just another way to work creatively.

*(Work in your notebook)*

Is there anyone in your neighborhood you see regularly but don't know? Like a woman walking her dog, or a grandfather through the window of apartment across the street? **Make up the life story of this person** and surprise yourself.

*(Work in your notebook)*

Make up someone who's in the **Guinness Book of World Records** for something outrageous. Name the character and describe him or her physically. Did your character hold the most olive pits in his mouth, or carry the world's heaviest book bag the farthest or spit higher in the air than anyone else? How would the character's life change after being listed in the Record Book?

*(Work in your notebook)*

Invent a person with **animal characteristics**. Don't be too obvious ("She had big, floppy ears like a rabbit"). Instead, subtly describe a behavior that can remind the reader of an animal. Perhaps this person has a way of crinkling her nose, or lifting her head and sniffing the air. It works best not to mention the animal involved. Try not to give too many hints, either. If your character swings upside down from trees and eats bananas, everyone will guess it's a ---

*"Goldfish."*

*"Yes, Nardo. You don't miss a trick."*

Write a story based on a bag of **groceries**. The items you bought may be characters having a conversation. What would they be hoping for or arguing about? Maybe, the empty grocery bag is empty. Does someone use it to carry a present to a birthday party? Is the bag used to clean up dog poop in the street? Does your brother blow air into it and then pop it to scare you? What happens after that?

*(Work in your notebook)*

Write a story about a world where **shoes**, boots and sandals are the characters. How is a sneaker different from a flip-flop? What sort of voice would a thigh-high suede boot have, compared to an old hiking boot?

*(Work in your notebook)*

This one is for Ari and Rachel in Bethesda, Maryland. Imagine a world where the "people" are **drinks**. Your characters can be juice, soda, coffee, tea, water or wine. Find a distinct personality for each type of beverage. Are beer and milk friends? They're not? But nutritionists say they're both "superfoods." What about tomato juice and grape juice, or coffee and root beer? Set your story anywhere: A place with lots of drinks, or a place where it's hard to find one. Do any of them spill? Does that hurt them or does it tickle?

*(Work in your notebook)*

Write a story with characters that are **bathing suits**. How does the personality of swimming trunks differ from that of a string bikini or a racing suit?

*(Work in your notebook)*

Invent characters you'd find in a **laundry** hamper. Are some cleaner than others? Are some not even clothes, and there by mistake? Imagine an important receipt or half a sandwich.

***"I thought I smelled peanut butter and honey!"***

*(Work in your notebook)*

Now, get inside an object's "head." Choose **a pillow, a fountain pen, a towel, a tongue** or something else. Does your character think and speak in English? Maybe the towel speaks "Towelese"! Was the pillow born in Pufflesberg?

## WRITE ABOUT AND DRAW YOUR "CHARACTER"

*(Work in your notebook)*

Other places to find **inanimate characters** (objects, to which you give thoughts and feelings): A front closet, a bottom drawer or a gardening shed. Think of more places to find inanimate characters:

*(Work in your notebook)*

**Develop your characters** (those based on objects as well as those based on living things) by showing how they **relate to others**.

Write about two characters on a **trip together**. Where are they going and why? Are they friends, strangers or relatives? How old? Is it a good trip or a bad one? Is it boring or exciting? Describe each character's experience.

*(Work in your notebook)*

Now consider **two travelers who part ways**. Are they backpacking students, retirees or business people? Describe why they separate and what happens to each of the characters during the first day that follows.

*(Work in your notebook)*

Set a story in a **workplace**, and include any two characters you might find there. They can be employees or customers, repairmen, executives or civil servants. How do they relate to each other? Can they express themselves freely in this workplace, or do they have to stay reserved? Or, might some of them have more fun at work than they do at home?

*(Work in your notebook)*

Write a story about one character who spends money as if **he's rich, and becomes poor**, and another character who spends money as if **he's poor, and becomes rich**. Do they ever cross paths? Is one happier than the other? Which of your characters is a nicer person, or are they equally nice? Remember, there's no single right answer.

*(Work in your notebook)*

Now, think some more about "wealth" and imagine a rich character with a **poor** life, or a poor character with a **rich** life.

They aren't necessarily enemies. Make their relationship unexpected. What if the rich character is vegetarian and gets upset when the poor one kills a bug outside?

*(Work in your notebook)*

Opposites are interesting. Now, invent a character that finds **exciting things boring** and another character that finds **boring things exciting**. Are they friends?

*(Work in your notebook)*

You can also create one character that **yells** while another **whispers** or one who **drags** himself along, while the other **prances**, or one with **bad manners** while another is **polite**. Try to give them interesting relationships, without making obvious choices (the one who yells doesn't have to be angry, the one who prances need not be happy and the one with poor manners might be very nice otherwise)

*(Work in your notebook)*

*What is it now, Nardo? Can't you let people get through this book in peace? What?! No, someone is not "copying your paper." They can't see you. How can a snake write anyway? There is NOT a pen in your mouth... Are you even enrolled in this workshop?*

Please remember that when someone else uses the same idea you're working on, you each produce something different. People see things in their own way, so no one can really "steal" someone else's idea for writing. It's the same with drawing. Two people can draw a snake, but each drawing will look different.

*"Even if it's the most handsome snake in the universe."*

*"You're shedding, Nardo."*

Do you know anyone who acts **one way in front of adults and another way in front of kids**? Maybe it's a giggling Goody Goody who jumps through hoops to please the adults but then becomes a spiteful Bossy Britches when she's with kids her age. Or maybe it's a teacher who acts joyous and childlike with her students, but becomes a dull, withdrawn wallflower with other grown-ups.

**WRITE ABOUT AND DRAW YOUR CHARACTER** *in your notebook*

Now, create another character that has **dual behaviors**, depending on who's around her/him. Show **how the character changes** from one behavior to the other, by using body language in addition to dialogue. This is a hard one. If you try it, please stand in front of your mirror and cheer.

*(Work in your notebook)*

Invent a **new sort of Pinocchio**. Instead of having his nose grow when he tells a lie, he or she will have something happen each time he or she behaves in a certain way. Maybe each time she scratches her head, her foot vibrates, or each time he whistles, his ears wiggle. You decide what happens after which behavior, and how it affects his or her life.

*(Work in your notebook)*

Take **two colors** and make them into characters. Where do they live and what do they want out of life? Would navy blue and mauve be friends? Why or why not? Does one love tap dancing while the other only cares about riding a unicycle?

## WRITE ABOUT YOUR COLORS, THEN MAKE A COLLAGE *in your notebook*

Create two characters. **One's an artist, and one is not.** How are they different? People often answer that the artist is messier and has her head in the clouds. She forgets appointments and is unconventional. But what if it's the other way around and the artist is on time and traditional, while the non-artist is the non-conformist who comes late? Try to get inside their heads so you go beyond: "Morgan made an exquisite and groundbreaking painting, while Surya organized her closet then balanced her checkbook."

*(Work in your notebook)*

Write a scene between a **cartoon character** you invent and a **live action** character. The action need not be cartoon action with "zooms", "boings" and "pows". How do they speak and what do they feel? Draw your cartoon character, then write your scene.

*(Work in your notebook)*

Bring more dimensions to your characters, by finding some **good qualities in a character you dislike and some weaknesses in a character you do like.** Maybe the character you don't like is based on a mean kid at school who turns out to be very kind to animals. The character you do like might be based on a friend who's unreliable. She'll ask you to sleep over and then invite someone else instead. What if the disliked character evolves into the hero of your next story?

**WRITE ABOUT THE GOOD IN A BAD CHARACTER
AND VICE VERSA** *in your notebook*

You're getting to be a character expert! Now, **invent a character
that invents a character**! This doesn't necessarily need to be a
writer, does it? What about Geppetto, who made a puppet that
became a boy? Try to make your character as original as possible,
and the same goes for the character he or she invents.

*(Work in your notebook)*

**Conflict** can inspire a story. Differences of opinion can be as
fascinating as differences in appearance or upbringing. Even
people who seem the same can have opposite points of view.
Identical twins might be in conflict about which guests to invite
to their Halloween party guests and what theme they'll have.
Think of some other situations, then

**WRITE A STORY IN WHICH TWO CHARACTERS ARE
IN CONFLICT.**

*(Work in your notebook)*

Now, think some more about **opposing qualities**. Imagine a
character that is **weak** in one way (physically or morally) in a
scene with a character that is **strong** in some way (strong willed

or muscle bound). Consider a character that's relaxed while another is tense, or one that's an introvert (shy) while another is an extrovert (outgoing). Often, people aren't really the way they appear. Someone who seems very smart can actually turn out to be less so, just as someone who appears not so smart can turn out to be highly intelligent. What other examples can you list?

**WRITE ABOUT TWO CHARACTERS WITH UNEXPECTED DIFFERENCES** *in your notebook*

You might also explore the idea of **a character that's too honest**, to the point of being annoying, or making normal people feel like thieves. He'd refuse raises, turn down paid hotels by his company when he works late, and decline free lunches. He'd make trouble in the name of virtue. Put him in a story with **a compulsive liar** or a con artist, and see what happens.

**WRITE ABOUT AN HONEST CHARACTER AND A DISHONEST CHARACTER** *in your notebook*

Next, go in-depth and invent a character that acts one way, but is a completely different person on the inside. Do you know anyone who seems ultra-confident, but who is really insecure deep down? Someone who complains constantly, but on the inside is actually sweet and agreeable? Or someone who seems brave on the outside but is really a coward? **Invent a character that looks one way but is secretly different**.

*(Work in your notebook)*

**Love and hate** are such powerful emotions, they can overwhelm us. Choose something or someone you really love and something or someone you completely despise. Put the two in a story together and see how interesting it is when they mingle. Does the kid you have a crush on like to eat kim chi, which you can't stand? Do you see someone you hate being around wearing the exact same t-shirt you bought using eight months of your pocket money? Are you at the movies, and see your best friend and worst enemy sitting together, sharing a large popcorn? Remember, if you're interested in someone, you can't really "hate" him or her, can you? And don't the people you love sometimes get on your nerves? The more you write and think the more you'll see the two emotions are complex and intertwined.

*(Work in your notebook)*

Try inventing the most **boring character** ever, but be sure to make your story or description **interesting**. Does your **drawing** of the character have to be boring, too? Of course not. It may take a very detailed drawing to capture just the right boring aspects to make your character as interesting to look at as he or she is to read about!

**WRITE AN INTERESTING STORY ABOUT A BORING CHARACTER** *in your notebook*

Now that you can creative interesting characters, try writing a story with **no characters**. One student argued it couldn't be done. Cathy asked her to try it, anyway. She wrote a good story that day.

**WRITE A STORY WITH NO CHARACTERS** *in your notebook*

# CHAPTER 3:

# ADD NOURISHING THOUGHTS

This chapter is about the **HOW** and the **WHAT** of your stories: **style and plot**; the path your main character takes, and how you describe it to your reader. You'll see that a well defined character will have clear reactions that will help determine your plot. But first, think about some aspects of style.

**Point of view ("POV")** is an incredibly powerful tool in writing. It allows you to get inside someone's head and see the world through their eyes. What would the Wizard of Oz be like if the story was told entirely from Toto's POV? It might start *"While waiting for the girl with the basket to come home from school today, I managed to steal some slop from the pigs. Boy, was that good....Then, I chased the chickens and dug up a few rose bushes...."*

When you write a story, think about how it will be told. Will you choose a third person's (or narrator's) point of view? You can also narrate in the first person, from the main character or another character's POV. If you write a story about a shoe, you can imagine the shoe wearer's point of view, a narrator's, an observer's, or even the POV of some gunk you have sticking to the sole. These can all work.

**CHOOSE A CHARACTER'S POV, then write and illustrate a STORY ABOUT A SHOE**

*(Work in your notebook)*

Write from the POV of something in the **dining room** during a meal. Will you choose a lit candlestick? A chair cushion? A stain on the ivory linen tablecloth? A cracker crumb on the rug?

**WRITE A STORY OR DESCRIPTION and illustrate it** *in your notebook*

Write and/or illustrate a story from the POV of an item inside **a purse**. Is it a coin, a tissue, a lipstick, a mirror, a photo or a bus ticket?

*(Work in your notebook)*

Now, go inside the stem of a **houseplant**. Is it thinking *"I'm drowning! Can't they stop watering me?"* or *"I'm desperate for a drink. Can't they see my drying, droopy leaves?"*

**WRITE A POV OF A HOUSEPLANT**

*(Work in your notebook)*

Write a story from an **inanimate object**'s POV as it "watches" someone eat a meal in a diner. Is your inanimate object the counter, the salt shaker or the waiter's apron's POV?

*(Work in your notebook)*

Write from the POV of an inanimate object in a **bathroom**, when someone comes to come hair or brush teeth. How might the shower curtain or the mirror comment about this visit...?

*(Work in your notebook)*

Now try writing from the POV of a **broom**. Is it a broom that sweeps up hair at the barber shop, or a broom backstage in a theatre?

*(Work in your notebook)*

Create two very **different characters** and, using POV, write how each one would react to missing a plane, breaking a crystal glass at someone's house, eating the last brownie before the only person who didn't get one arrives too late to claim it.

*(Work in your notebook)*

Get inside the mind of someone completely different from you. A 10 year old boy might write from the POV of a blind, **90 year old woman**. Try hard to think what life is like for that person. If you have no idea, make it up. That's what you're here for!

Write a scene from the POV of a **cab driver**, and then the **passenger**. Your characters may have conflicting feelings and desires, or similar ones. Do the same for **waiter and customer**, thief and victim, hen and hatching egg, **jailer and prisoner**, coach and athlete, homeless person and soup kitchen volunteer. Was the homeless person once rich? Is the volunteer actually poor? Or from the family that caused the homeless person to lose his wealth?

If you choose someone shopping for clothes and the person who works in the clothing store, describe each of their feelings. Maybe the **shopper** thinks everything is the perfect color and style, but doesn't like the way the clothes fit. Maybe the **salesperson** knows this is a customer who tries on 20 items, leaves them in a heap in the dressing room and buys nothing.

Make your choices as original as you can. This exercise can also be done using inanimate objects. The **bathtub and the bather**, the razor and the face being shaved, the steering wheel and the driver of the car...

*(Work in your notebook)*

## ALL ABOUT HER (or him)

Invent a female character, then describe her from the **points of view of three other characters**, male or female, that you'll create. They can be close friends or family, or observe her from afar. How do they feel about her? The exercise can also be done with a male character.

*"Or a dashing snake, loved by all."*

*"If you insist."*

*(Work in your notebook)*

POV provides the reader with something vital: **perspective.** A blade of grass may be insignificant to us, but to an ant, it might seem like a highway. **Write something from the POV of a small character, or the POV of an enormous character, then draw your character.**

*(Work in your notebook)*

Over **time,** different characters view the same events with different perspectives. Invent two friends, siblings or coworkers who are together for a stretch of time, then write each of their separate memories about that period, years later. Do they see things the same way, or differently?

*(Work in your notebook)*

*XkLLNEosbche vosxseb qsjdyurns,ruqbq Sheez nhot at ze keebowrd. NARDO curnn CAN toop, tyrp, TYPE!!!*

*"Cathy's not here, readers. Must be writer's block. Never fear! I will gallantly step in:"*

*"Invent five good reasons for not writing anything, ever. 'Because my finger hurts' is much too simple. Try:*

*'A raccoon broke into my house and knocked a vase off the high shelf. As I tried to catch it, I bumped the top of the piano which slammed down on my hand. The vase shattered on the floor. My hand throbbed red like something in a cartoon. With my other hand, I grabbed the glue to repair it, but had to use my mouth to open the tube and then my lips stuck together. Crying because my hand hurt so much made my glued lips start bleeding. Our dog started barking at the raccoon, and the neighbors called 911.....(Start scribbling in those notebo--*

*"Hey, is that a NET? No! Back off!*
*MMMMMMPhhhhhhhzzzzzzZZZZZ."*

*It's okay, everyone. Nardo's asleep. Sorry for the interruption. (He told Cathy there was a reporter from Time Magazine was waiting downtown to interview her and she fell for it.)*

*Before getting back to writing styles, why not play with Nardo's idea about good excuses not to write? If you make them creative enough, then you ARE writing!*

## LIST FIVE CREATIVE REASONS FOR NOT WRITING.

*(Work in your notebook)*

Sometimes, instead of following an assignment, students work "next to it"; using part of the instructions but discarding the rest. They may still end up with interesting results, but they miss the intended creative exercise. When a student hasn't grasped an assignment, Cathy might wonder **"What were your ears doing?"** Were they in the glove compartment of a Ferrari? Were they boating on the Seine? Come up with some creative reasons your ears might not capture an assignment.

*(Work in your notebook)*

## STYLE YOUR WORDS

You can try different hairstyles, so why not try different writing styles? Some authors are at their best describing intricate settings and behaviors, while keeping dialogue to a minimum. Others do the opposite. Certain writers relate every detail of their characters' thoughts, while some devote all their energy to action sequences. All these approaches can lead to excellent, original work. The next exercises introduce many **different stylistic effects**. Experiment with them, and see which ones you enjoy using the most.

## NON-VERBAL

Think about what **non-verbal** exchanges could take place between characters. Remember, non-verbal means communication without words, also called "body language". What does a shrug tell you, or the shake of a head, a nod, or sneer? How does arrogance look, or shame, hate, love or anger?

Maybe your characters are unable to talk, or maybe they just can't talk where they are. Maybe one character is an animal, and the communication, with a human or another animal has no words. Or maybe your characters are two aliens who live on a planet with no speech at all, just gestures. Now, experiment with non-verbal communication between two characters.

*(Work in your notebook)*

**Stream of consciousness** *is a kind of writing without punctuation where you just let all your ideas flow the way someone would speak without waiting for anyone else to answer if you see a bird over there you might write hey look a bird is that a robin or a sparrow.* Some entire books are written in stream of consciousness. They have a very immediate feel, since it's just like being in the character's head. Stream of consciousness is a real change of pace.

Try writing a stream of consciousness paragraph for a character who's **a marathon runner, or a Halloween pumpkin** about to be carved, or someone who wakes up in a hospital with both arms and legs in casts. Let your reader feel the exhaustion, anxiety or boredom the characters experience, by the words you choose.

*(Work in your notebook)*

You can also try your own stream of consciousness in these situations: You wake up late for school, get to the airport late to make a flight, or **you're on a blind date**, smiling on the outside but with a turmoil of thoughts racing through your mind. Start at any point in the story: The alarm could be broken, and another noise wakes you, or you're frantically getting dressed, or you're sweating as you charge down the street...

*(Work in your notebook)*

Another stream of consciousness exercise presents your **life story** via a series of pictures you describe. You can consider any memory you have as a "photo" or picture. The biography moves quickly, as you skip through time. For example:

*"Round faced toddler in a high chair, white cotton pajamas with snaps. She's raising a bowl of cereal high above her head....little girl with a puppy on her lap, snapping at her. She looks surprised, the flowers behind her wilting, late summer...."*

Now, consider **comic** and **tragic stories**. A comic story may make you laugh out loud, or just smile to yourself, via humor that's slapstick, ironic, absurd, or somewhere in between. Do you think the characters have to be funny, or could they also be serious, if the situation is funny? Would it be possible to have a comic story in a tragic setting? What about a tragic story in a comic setting? If something sad happens to a comedian, could that be funny, would it be sad or both? A tragic story can make you sad, so avoid writing one unless you need a good cry. But if the ending gives the reader hope for the future, writing a tragic story can become a very positive experience!

**Write a comic or tragic story in your notebook.**

Think of a few **situations that combine comic and tragic aspects**. A circus clown attending a funeral in costume, an employee in a prison, waiting to throw the switch to the electric chair, reading a comic book and giggling. Could each of these situations lead to a comic story as well as a tragic one?

There's a lot of tension in sad situations, just as there is in comic ones. Crying is a way to release that tension, but so is laughter. Sometimes, people laugh so hard, they start crying, or cry so hard, they start laughing. Matthew couldn't stop laughing at his grandfather's funeral when he was four years old. Naomi cries when she hears certain music, and then starts laughing at how silly it is to be crying.

Tragedy and comedy may seem to be at opposite ends of the spectrum, but there are lots of nuances of each. Try writing a story that has both elements, and notice when tragedy crosses over and becomes comedy and vice versa.

*(Work in your notebook)*

**Exaggeration** is a great way to loosen up and enjoy writing. Take something that really happened at school or during a vacation, or something you invent, and describe it in as outlandish and farfetched way as possible. If you got up one morning, you can rewrite that to be:

 *"I shot out of bed, a flaming arrow"* or *"I defied gravity, leaping from my mattress like an Olympian."*

***Looks as if someone else is waking up, too: Nardo, everyone's favorite creative constrictor!***

***Why is it that no doctor has ever detected him during Cathy's medical check-ups? As soon as she's home, so is Sir Snake. Where do you think Nardo goes to hide from the world? Under Cathy's bed? Or does he pack a duffle and leave town? DESCRIBE HOW AND WHERE NARDO GOES and be sure to exaggerate!***

*(Work in your notebook)*

Significantly **exaggerate** something you did recently and write a short description, no holds barred. You didn't eat half a sandwich, you gorged on an entire roasted pig! You slid the contents of the salad bar into a large funnel placed halfway down your throat! Instead of getting some change from the jar in your room, you held up a bank....

Compare *"Today I got up after my alarm went off. I had breakfast, put on my makeup, and took the bus to work"* with: *"My alarm clanged like fire engine sirens, jolting me awake. I staggered to my feet, feeling as if a cast iron frying pan was banging my brain. I slurped and crunched down a breakfast of sawdust and supersonic sugar. Outraged at my boss, I slashed on my war paint, and then stormed to the bus stop. Out of my way, world!..."*

*(Work in your notebook)*

Exaggeration gives you a sense of **proportion**. Now, invent a character that exaggerates the importance of a **tiny detail** while underplaying something more important. Take a trip, during which your character glosses over the fact she was invited to the Palace of Brunei, only to rant and rave about a dead fly she found on the private tennis court. What does this tell you about her?

*(Work in your notebook)*

Another way to make your writing more interesting is to use **juxtaposition**, or opposing concepts.

Compare *"The farmer worked in the fields for 10 hours"* to *"From the first shaft of morning light to the last glimmer at dusk, the farmer toiled in his fields, the lone vertical being in a waving, horizontal sea of wheat."* You get a fuller picture, don't you?

With juxtaposition, something good can seem even better when you compare it to something bad. Cool spring water seems even more pure and refreshing if you compare it to tepid water that comes out of a rusty pump. Try using **opposites** as you describe the great and terrible things at a real or an imaginary **camp**.

*(Work in your notebook)*

Describe something you **experience often**, such as falling asleep, drinking a glass of milk, going for a bike ride, watching the sunset, putting your shoes on, waking up, and do so in two ways, one brief and to the point, the other more elaborate. The longer version can contain emotions and speculation in addition to more details. Here's an example from "Juicy Brain", age 9:

Long:

*"I watch my arm extend, my hand reaching. Brushing against the wall, my fingers sense a bump. They pass over it and move again on the smooth wallpaper. Finding the bump again, they press it briefly, then let go. Golden, glowing light floods the room."*

Short:

*"I flick on the light."*

*(Work in your notebook)*

You may need relief from the more complicated exercises. Time for **THE ATTACK OF THE MONKEY BUTTS!** Are the characters monkeys with normal monkey butts, or humans or aliens with monkey butts? Where do they come from? Buttsylvania? Outer space? Whom do they attack? Whose side are you on and who wins?

**"I do. With my army of Snaky Butts!"**

**"Good luck, Nard. And watch out for flying banana peels."**

*(Work in your notebook)*

## SYMPATHETIC LANDSCAPE

This wonderful stylistic element of Victorian Literature is used to let what a character feels color his or her environment. If a heroine is upset, and runs away from a mansion weeping, chances are the skies will cloud up and start storming. If a character is overjoyed, the sky may be bright blue with fluffy, white cotton clouds. A depressed character might look around and see wilted plants and lethargic creatures around him, under a heavy, grey sky.

Create **sympathetic landscapes** for a character that has a jealous rage, a character that's absentminded, or a character that laughs hysterically. Now try doing so for an insane murderer, a loving nanny, or a strict prison guard.

*(Work in your notebook)*

**Style** refers not only to your descriptions but also to the way characters **speak and think**. Take a body part and add an adjective. It doesn't have to be alliterative, like the Noble Nostril or the Bemused Behind. It can be the Troubled Elbow or the Happy Ankle. Now give that character a distinctive way of thinking or speaking. Is the voice babyish? Pompous? Optimistic? Riddled with slang? Now, let this character narrate your story.

*"How about Gallant Guts?"*

*"Anything's possible. Did you win your battle with the Monkey Butts?"*

*"No. They cheated."*

*(Work in your notebook)*

Cathy does have to give Nardo some credit. If she's too focused on one assignment, he distracts her so she can move on to something else. Sometimes, he cheers her up when she feels alone. There's more to him than she thought.

Look at some stories you've written so far. Does each character have a distinct point of view and **"voice"**? Try altering the voice of one of your minor characters, given him or her a new way of expressing his or her personality. How does it change your story?

## DIALOGUE

Your characters may have a style of speaking, a certain vocabulary or an accent. WHAT they say is as important as HOW they say it. Dialogue should sound like what real people say, and not be used to catch up on details the reader can't gather from your text.

Consider:

*"Oh, so being chased by the mean dog owned by the lady who runs the flower shop was the reason Olivia's cousin Jonathan kept coming late to Backgammon Club events, not having to take care of his ant farm, as was previously believed!"*

There is a way to impart all the above information in a more natural and entertaining way, as things happen, rather than by swallowing it whole, after the fact.

Characters' conversations should move your story forward, not grind it to a halt. The following only works if characters are just learning English or overly awkward.

*"Yo."*

*"Hey."*

*"What's going on?"*

*"Not much."*

*"Feel like doing anything?"*

*"I don't know. How about you?"*

*"We could just take turns saying boring things."*

*"Sounds good. You start."*

The exercises that follow are designed to get you thinking about **interesting** things your characters could say, in situations in which something is actually happening.

Write how someone who is **late** speaks to various people he or she meets while rushing to his or her destination. (Note, there's no time to dawdle over phrases that don't get right to the point! Your character has to be clear and express urgency. Up to you if this is done politely or abruptly.)

*(Work in your notebook)*

You're in a department store fitting room and hear sobbing in the room next to you, as a person talks into a cell phone. **Write the part of the conversation you overhear**.

*(Work in your notebook)*

Write a description of a parade, a banquet or a car accident in the **"voice"** of a teenager, then repeat the exercise using the "voice" of a grandfather, a non-native English speaker or a four year old. How does the narrator's vocabulary change? Is one account duller than the others? Why would it be so? Rework your descriptions until they sound natural to you.

*(Work in your notebook)*

Write a dialogue between two characters of the same age that have very **different voices**. Maybe one character uses slang words while the other doesn't even use contractions (for example, "do not" instead of "don't"). What other ways might speech differ between two people?

*(Work in your notebook)*

Now, write a dialogue between two **inanimate objects**. How does the "voice" of a jewelry box compare to that of a compass?

*(Work in your notebook)*

Just as an artist pays great attention to what he sees, a writer needs to notice the details of anything around his characters. Doing the next exercises will improve your powers of observation.

## DESCRIPTIVE WRITING

Great descriptive writing provides a detailed look and feel of a setting, character or event. Readers will "be there" thanks to fresh and compelling words.

Contrast *"She poured the water into a glass"* with *"The cool, crystal stream danced through the sunlight, splashing drops like diamonds onto the silky skin on her delicate hand."*

Another style of descriptive writing might use plainer language, but still concentrate on every detail: *"The water pitcher was heavy, wobbling as she lifted it. Her hand was small, her fingers thin. She picked up a glass with her other hand, held it at a slight angle, and poured. Water rushed into the glass, but none spilled. She smiled, relieved this task was now over. She put the pitcher down carefully and handed me the glass."*

Consider **detailed descriptions** of simple actions, like picking up your mail, making a phone call or preparing a sandwich. You can either carefully describe each step of the action, or use **metaphors** and **similes** to elaborate your descriptions. That is, make comparisons that help the reader feel and see what you're writing about: The soft silk that is a puppy's ear; a smile as dazzling as a sunburst; a sweet baby, like honey in a blanket. Metaphors make what you describe equal to something else:

"Sharing is the road to friendship" and similes are approximations, using "like" or "as". Strive to invent some that have never been heard before. Instead of "Gentle as a lamb" you might try "Gentle as a soft boiled egg" and renew "Rough as sandpaper" to "Rough as a cyclone of pebbles." Make up a few more:

*(Work in your notebook)*

You can also use **metaphors** to describe words in a fresh way: "Cruelty" could be defined as "Launching mean words from a sling shot, "Isolation" could be "Being sent to jail on Mars," and strenuous exercise could be "Having your drumming heart try to exit your body via your mouth." Find more "definitions" for "Joy," "Surprise," "Envy" and "Sleep".

*(Work in your notebook)*

**Invent or use atypical words** to describe the intense feeling of being hungry, tired, bored, nauseous or itchy (One student, Raphinké, coined "thirstarving" to connote dire thirst),. If you choose hunger, try to avoid clichés such as "I'm so famished, I could eat a horse!" Be innovative instead: *"Digestive acids ate into my stomach lining like bleach cleaner. I saw a stale cake crumb on a tray and began to drool...."*

*(Work in your notebook)*

In addition to physical feelings, consider some emotions. Invent phrases to describe happiness (*"pink flamingos waltzed in my heart"*?) frustration (*"my brain cells popped like bubble wrap"*?), fury, elation, despair....

*(Work in your notebook)*

Describe roughness, softness, brightness or darkness in detail. Involve every sense you can. **What's the feel, smell, taste and**

**look of each of these things?** This is a poetic exercise, and you can absolutely decide what brightness tastes like.

Lemon? Berries? Ice? What does darkness smell like? Moth balls? Grandpa's old shirts? A coal cellar?

*(Work in your notebook)*

Describe a rainstorm without using the words "rain", "drop" or "storm" or a snowstorm without using the words "snow", "flake" or "storm". Can the clouds drench you with torrents of icy wetness? Can the sky blind you with cold, fluffy fallout? Your turn.

*(Work in your notebook)*

Now, describe someone who is **average** in every respect, without using the words "average," "typical" or "usual". Try "bland," "invisible" or other, different words.

*(Work in your notebook)*

Describe a **sunset** and make it as corny as you can. Be sure to jam in as many clichés as possible *("So long, lowering fireball in the serene sky! Serenaded with pastels from celestial palettes, you'll sleep soundly, an innocent babe swaddled in cottony clouds. See you at the crack of dawn when the cock crows and the early bird gets up to catch the worm!")*. Read over what you wrote, then try to make it even worse. This will make you aware of using unoriginal phrases, and may leave you proud you have the skill to write something bad on purpose!

*(Work in your notebook)*

Choose one thing you do to get ready in the morning, and **describe it in detail**, with respect to each of your senses. If you're eating toast, describe the sounds, smell, taste, look and feel. Include what sort of plate or napkin you're using, what table or counter it's on, the light in the kitchen, or anything else closely involved with the event.

*(Work in your notebook)*

What original set of words can you find to **describe the feeling** of doing a good deed? Is it like "caramel sunshine with a side order of singing canaries" or is it like "a shower of marigolds"? How about feeling guilty when you do something you know you shouldn't. Is it "a dark shadow, with vultures circling above" or perhaps "an anvil about to fall on your head"? Now describe feeling nervous and jumpy, or too full after a big meal.

*Cathy has never seen Nardo with such a bulging belly in the middle of the morning. And she can't find her left slipper. Odd.....*

*(Work in your notebook)*

Work with **an unusual emotion**, such as emptiness. It's different from sadness, loneliness, boredom, isn't it? Describe how emptiness feels, in a paragraph written from your own POV, or that of a character you invent.

*(Work in your notebook)*

Write a scene in which a character is both **hot and cold.** This can occur in any season. Describe where and how it happens and especially how your character feels.

*(Work in your notebook)*

How does it feel when a **friendship is forming vs. when it's dissolving**? Be as detailed as possible. When it's forming, is there a moment when you can take things for granted? That your friend will save you a seat at lunch or be available for sleepovers on weekends? When the friendship starts to disintegrate, is there one disappointing day when you see none of your usual patterns are upheld? Is the disintegration gradual, is it all over quickly or does it depend?

*(Work in your notebook)*

Describe in detail **eating something you love.** Then describe **eating something you hate.** Be sure to avoid the obvious: "Eggplant tastes disgusting and makes me want to throw up", find more expressive words: "A slimy slug went down my throat and almost out my nose. It's spongy grey and sopping with grease…"

*(Work in your notebook)*

Here's another way to use your descriptive skills: A character enters a room and the only information we get comes from the **non-verbal reactions, or body language** of others already there. For example, if the new person enters the waiting room in a bus station and smells particularly bad, a woman sitting on a bench might hold a handkerchief to her nose, or move away, or roll her eyes.

*(Work in your notebook)*

Pick another setting and different characters, and see what sort of **body language** you can describe. Maybe a popular boy comes to sit at the counter of a restaurant, while a group of girls watch him from a booth. Or a woman is talking too loudly on her cell phone in a store, and bothering other shoppers.

*(Work in your notebook)*

*"That big blabber didn't have to start pointing at me and screaming in the middle of Nordstrom. It was HER earring that kept knocking me in the face on the escalator."*

*"So you swallowed it. Nice going."*

*(Can't take that snake anywhere!)*

## MANAGE YOUR PLOT TO GROW SOLID STORIES

It will come as no news to you that stories need a beginning, middle and end to make sense. In the same way, an insect needs a head, thorax and abdomen. If they're not in that order, it just doesn't work, right? Well, it's truer in the case of the insect.

**Stories can be disassembled and put back together in a different order**, without falling apart! Before you write and prove it, consider some examples.

Ever read a book written in **flashback**? Of course you have. One gripping opening might be:

*"Jane put on her purple jacket, looked in the mirror and fluffed up her hair. She had no idea it was the last day of her life."*

Then the story backs up so readers get to know Jane way before her last day alive. The author puts the end at the beginning, or more precisely, makes the end into the beginning. Thinking of parts of stories as removable makes it easier to try different structures, and be more creative. Try starting Jane's story from another point; when her family moves to a new city, when she graduates from college, or when she's hit by the fateful rickshaw.

*(Work in your notebook)*

Think of a story you know well and try to **change the order of its parts**. What if the Wizard of Oz started in Oz, and went back to Kansas much later? That could be interesting. Or The Little Mermaid could start with Ariel walking on land, before she becomes a mermaid and meets King Triton, her father, under the sea. Sometimes, it doesn't take much smoothing after you change the order in your story, and the results can make your work more exciting.

*(Work in your notebook)*

What's important when you're cutting and pasting, is to **keep the story moving at all times**. Readers only need a bit of explanation to stay with a story, so don't add so much that things slow down.

You can include any offbeat events and reactions that occur to you, as long as you find a way they can make sense. If you write:

*"One day, Balboa the Toad crashed into a guava and robbed a casino"* you'd better follow up on all those events, and develop a logic that makes them possible. Was he peddling a bike or driving a car that crashed into a guava? You know that toads can't do either, but you can decide that in your story they can and explain how. It may also take some work to describe how a toad robs a casino. But if you find an interesting way a reader is willing to believe, there's no way he'll put your book down. **This is what creative thinking is all about.**

Work carefully when you come close to the ending. Stories that end too abruptly aren't worthy of their beginnings. "Then, everyone died" may get a laugh in your writing group, but more than anything, it says: "I couldn't find a way to finish my story, and this was the fastest way out." It's like ducking out and not keeping your promises.

A dance teacher shared this secret: When you do a plié (that's a knee bend, for all you guys who play rugby), don't think "down" even though your body lowers as you bend your knees. Think "up" which will remind you to stretch tall. This makes the movement more graceful and less predictable.

*"I'm always graceful, and never predictable."*

*This is what Nardo always says when he slithers up to steal sesame crackers from Cathy's desk.*

*"Mwah buy you anuffer one."*

*"Don't talk with your mouth full."*

You can use the same reasoning for writing an ending. If you think "beginning" you'll **open doors to more original ideas**, instead of shutting things down with an obvious resolution. A writer can end a story with **questions**, and speculate about the future, leaving some things open. Although readers will want major issues resolved, tying up every single loose end is not always necessary.

In solving the central problem, remember your solution need not be the expected one. You can also solve one problem and introduce another one at the end, suggesting the story isn't really over, it's just stopping here to let passengers off the train. The main character may not know what comes next, but he should feel he's reached a good point to take a break. This will leave your reader satisfied, too.

Go back to a story you had trouble ending, and **rewrite the end in your notebook**.

More classic advice is that the character is able to solve his problem himself, rather than get lucky. However, there's a lot you can do with luck. It's all in how the character reacts to his good or bad fortune that keeps our attention. If your character is well defined, you have what you need for a **solid story**.

*"Rock solid, with majestically strong, rippling muscles that----"*

*"Seen any lately?"*

No point in your story should be easy to guess. If you really want to write about a brave, handsome prince who saves a beautiful, imprisoned princess, after which they live happily ever after, try to give it a twist. Maybe she's really a Podiatrist, and he's the class coward. Take your mind somewhere completely new.

Other "easy" endings to avoid are making the whole story a dream, a film or a news broadcast. Why not brainstorm a few truly original endings now, even without a beginning? The main character can decide to move to the mountains, can shave her head or take up sky diving? Your turn.

*(Work in your notebook)*

**Backwards stories** take some engineering. Do they start at the end and go back in time until the beginning? Or do they necessarily need flashbacks to make sense? That is, do they need to go forward and then sometimes go back in time? Can you start by deciding on the character, his goal, how this goal is achieved and the ending, and then just fill those events in, in backwards chronology? Including dates could make it easier to follow. Thinking further, ask yourself if characters in a backwards story walk backwards and wear their clothes backwards? *A student in Cathy's high school class wore his jeans backwards, and probably won't mind if you include him as a character.* **Try writing a backwards story in your notebook**.

On to the **inside-out story**! Cathy wrote this on her "IDEAS" page without figuring out what it was....

...Okay, got it! This can be a story that starts in the middle, from the point of view of an element in the middle of the story: a character, the narrator or an object. Then it covers the outer edges, as if you could make the story into a three-dimensional folded paper structure. What parts would you see once the folds were there? This may be easier to do if you first write a simple story that goes forward, then really fold the paper and see what you get! Start with the inside (the middle of the story) and then write down the words you can see on the outside. This one's extra tricky, and calls for a round of applause if you complete it!

*(Work in your notebook)*

Imagine a strange force that **"hijacks"** your story and turns it into something completely different. When a story is hijacked, the narrator, action, characters or setting suddenly change wildly and with no apparent reason. But you still have to hold the story together! What happens can be preposterous or silly, but it has to make sense. You could start with a character that gets lost in a big city, but is next seen sitting in a field of daisies, having completely different goals. It's the same character, but a "hijacked" setting.

Or, you could keep the setting and hijack your character. A boy could wake up and be a little old lady instead, without remembering being a boy. Maybe other characters don't even ask the old lady where the boy went. Or, have the narrator suddenly turn against the author, you! That's hijacking, too. Try one now.

*(Work in your notebook)*

Another kind of hijacking is when the characters are aware of the narrator and fight with him/her. The author can also be targeted, since he's the person who created the narrator. Maybe the characters demand better treatment from the author, so go on strike. Perhaps a minor character organizes the strike, and then becomes a major character. Will the characters agree to stay in the story? How does the author react?

*(Work in your notebook)*

There's also the **sideways story.** Imagine a setting with three or four characters who don't all know each other, sitting in a row. It might be on a bench in a train station, or at a café, perhaps at tables like this:

Person A          People B and C                    Person D

Person D can't see Person A, but can see Person C and hear B and C talking. Person A can only see person B, but can hear B and C and can't see Person D.

Now, write the story from Person A's POV and then from Person D's POV, then intertwine them to make one, whole "sideways story". What truly happens and what does each observer presume happens? How different are A and D's observations and conclusions? Be sure to describe each of your characters. Are they around the same age and sex, or not?

*(Work in your notebook)*

Different from story hijacking is **a story within a story**. Start a first story with a character that goes off on a tangent. For example, the main character, a girl living on a farm, could have a problem getting along with her older sister. But we then get interested in the main character's collection of antique bracelets, so put the sister on hold. Either of the stories, the bracelets or the sister, should be able to stand alone, but you should also be able to fit one within the other and resolve both of them.

*(Work in your notebook)*

One way to do that is go back and forth between the "A" and "B" stories. If each chapter ends at a point where you can't wait to find out what happens next, then switch back to the other, which should be just as enthralling. This makes the reader even more eager to continue. It may sound complicated, but you can absolutely try to write a story within a story by yourself.

*(Work in your notebook)*

**SWERVING** lets an unexpected sequence take ALL the elements of your story in a new direction:

*"I put on my right sock, then I put on my left sock. I reached for my right shoe, then....a flaming arrow came throw the window and shot my painting of George Washington through the heart!"* Start a story and then take it on a swerve. Follow the sudden action that takes everything in a new direction, rather than end the sequence and go back to your socks. You can come back to them later, maybe after the whole adventure, when your main character notices he'd never put on his shoes! Try a swerving story.

*(Work in your notebook)*

Here's one dedicated to Nardo: Think of a something that could happen in the morning to **mess up your day**. Then, make it into a story. Does the day end up good or bad?

*(Work in your notebook)*

# CHAPTER 4:

## SPROUT A WRITING GROUP

You've noticed by now that there's a lot to keep track of when you write: your characters, setting, plot and style. Sometimes, working in pairs or in a group helps everyone improve faster. At least, you won't be lonely. You can exchange ideas, compare writing styles, and conquer stage fright when you read your work.

One of the best things about teaching creative writing is getting students to realize that reading something they don't like aloud to a group is not fatal. Not only do they survive, they become better writers!

You'll have plenty of turns being the listener when someone else reads something they think is pretty bad. You'll all learn to trust each other, and confidence will increase all around.

**GROUP WORKOUTS**

Write about the best feature of the person sitting across from you. Be original in the feature you choose and how you describe it. This person has probably heard she has rosy cheeks or big brown eyes before, so maybe you should choose her lower lip. Will you write about a boy's apricot ears, platypus feet, nose hairs as lush as Sherwood Forest, eyebrows as dense as a Persian carpet, or lashes as long as his fingers? Remember to keep your descriptions intriguing but not insulting. Otherwise, no one will be eager to write with you next time!

Reread the **Taravina** exercise in Chapter 2. Then assign each person in your group a function. One person could be the Minister of Tourism. She or he has to figure out how to get people to come visit Taravina. Another person could be the Culture Czar, in charge of the annual Festival. What do they celebrate? Independence from another country? Spring flowers? An indigenous animal? How is the town decorated? What are the songs and dances? What costumes are worn?

*(Work in your notebook)*

Another person runs the factory. What product do they manufacture? Someone else is the Head of Agriculture. What crops do they grow? Is it something special to their region, or something that grows in other countries? Someone else can be the chef at the top restaurant. What's the traditional meal served during the Festival?

*(Work in your notebook)*

On a day when your writing juices haven't started flowing, have each person **draw a picture**. The pictures can be realistic or abstract. Now pass your picture to someone else in the group and write a story inspired by the images on the page you were given. This is usually the jumpstart the group needs to get ideas into motion.

You can choose a photograph or painting in an **art book**, then either name and create the biographies of the characters, or, in the absence of characters, write a story set in the picture.

*(Work in your notebook)*

Write from the point of view of a **big toe** of a famous person. Each of you chooses someone different, and reveals who subtly. Consider the difference if you write "Stop strutting and shaking your hair and get on stage. They're waiting to hear 'Satisfaction'! rather than starting with "Guess what? I'm Mick Jagger's big toe!"

*(Work in your notebook)*

Have each person choose a noun, verb, adjective, article or adverb and then everyone helps write a sentence using all the words. Once you've agreed on the sentence, each of you will write a story and **place the sentence** at any point of the beginning, middle or end. Try to be surprising.

You can also work with:

*"This could take hours."*

*"Pretend it's not broken."*

*"Well, we didn't know."*

*"Six more, and you're out of here." (Note this can be positive or negative)*

*"These are not the right samples."*

*"I had that same blue sweater."*

*"You go first."*

*"Look what I found under the couch."*

*"Why are we whispering?"*

*"Stop those lemurs. They've got my-----"* (Here, you choose what they've taken from your character)

*"Only the Gubnarp was awake." (Be sure to describe the Gubnarp)*

*"Lift his head so it doesn't scrape the ground"*

*"This is supposed to be my room?"*

*"That baby looks worried."*

*"Don't open the second door."*

*"I need you to keep this for me."*

**"OR 'Nardo has just won the Nobel Prize for Literature.'"**

**"Great. Go ahead and break the news to Philip Roth."**

## WORD TRIGGERS

Another exercise to do in a group is to start with a **sound effect**: Sizzle, Crash, Zoom, Swoosh, Bang, Crack, Boom, Splash, Pop, etcetera, and see what story it inspires.

*(Work in your notebook)*

Write a story or poem inspired by **freshness**, either the behavior or about a substance. Consider a blade of grass, fresh coffee, innocence, fresh bread, rudeness or fresh air.

*(Work in your notebook)*

More word triggers are listed in Chapter 7.

What is **Merfnouk**? A new holiday? The latest dance? An item of clothing? A tasty, exotic dish? Invent and describe Merfnouk in as much detail as possible, then share all the different ideas in the group.

*(Work in your notebook)*

The **Revolution** is coming! Whether you chose the mice against the cats, the cockroaches against the apartment dwellers, or the thumbtacks against the thumbs, write an **official protest document** that includes demands for a better life. Be surprising and original. Be *orising* and s*urpriginal*!

*(Work in your notebook)*

Choose any two syllables, and combine them to make the name

of an **original product**. Assign a head of manufacturing, an advertising director, a research and development person (this is someone who might invent the next product in the line, if this one is a hit), factory workers, a head of sales, an editor of a consumer magazine who is against the product, and take it from there.

*(Work in your notebook)*

Play **Pass the Story.** The traditional way to do this is to have one person determine the setting, the next person determine the character and a problem, the next person try twice to solve it, and the last person bring a solution and describe how life has changed.

If you have nine people in your group, you can divide the parts like this: Physical description of the character, personality of the character, setting, an unexpected event, one character's reaction to that event, introduction of a new character, a new reaction, resolution, epilogue.

Pass the Story is a lot of fun, but a writing exercise you can take very seriously. It's very important to carefully read what the people before you wrote, so the story flows as smoothly as possible. Innovate, of course, but don't be silly for the sake of silliness. After some practice, you won't be able to tell when one writer stops and the next one starts. What teamwork! Try it.

*(Work in your notebook)*

*How quiet it gets when the writers concentrate and Nardo's not interrupting! (Could it be he's easily intimidated by talent?)*

The person who started the story reads it when it's finished, and everyone then discusses what they liked and how the stories might be improved. While it's all still fresh in your mind, note three ideas you could implement before the group meets again.

**Write your three ideas for improvement in your notebooks.**

**Oral Story Telling** is quite a skill. Some people invent extremely good stories on the spot, and have a flair for sharing them out loud. Other people stall the minute they have to speak in front of a group, even though their imaginations may take them on wonderful adventures on paper. This second kind of story makes excellent reading, but so do the first ones, as long as someone writes them down! Some people have a preference for oral or written story telling. See who in your writing group has a talent for which.

**Oral Story in a Group**: Go around the table and have each person add one thought to what was said by the person sitting on their right. Be sure to build on the story and not change it to something that doesn't connect. If you start:

*"Once there was a Countess named Julia"* the next person could say *"who could breathe fire"* and the next one *"to defend herself from a gorilla"* and the next one *"who wanted to steal her tiara."* It would not be a good idea to follow "the doorknob came off on the horse's neck" with "she took the orange juice and hurt the oak

tree" because no one would get anything out of that sequence. You may, however, note that for the **Bad Poetry Contest** in a later chapter!

*"Cathy can't just supply them with bad poetry then call it their contest! The kids are going to have to do their own terrible work, and then promise to get worse and worse forever!"*

*"Nardo, we never knew you had such a sense of fair play! You're an inspiration to reptiles!"*

**More group exercises:**

**Name the character** someone in the group describes, and try to be unexpected. If it's a bald guy, Fuzzy or Woolly could be surprising first names. If it's a blond supermodel, you could call her Thundy Frumpner.

*(Work in your notebook)*

**Describe the character** someone in the group names. Again, try to be surprising. If the character is called Elveena Witchpritchet, maybe you shouldn't give her a broom and a pointed hat. Or do so, but have her be synchronized swimmer or a pastry chef, not a sorceress.

*(Work in your notebook)*

Each person writes a **taste, sound, sight or texture** on separate slips of paper, then puts them into a bowl on the table. A second bowl contains each person's slips of paper with **characters, settings and situations**. Someone chooses one slip from each bowl, and everyone writes a story. If you get "starfish" and "a boy on stilts" you then decide where he is and what happens. With the prompts "fog horn" and "movie theatre" you'd invent the character and plot for the story. If "scratchy" and "marsh" are the cues, you'd come up with the plot and characters.

*(Work in your notebook)*

Each person writes a story that takes place in a **hair salon**, but from a different point of view. You might choose to be a customer of any age, male of female, a hair dresser, a person who shampoos the customers, the manager, a friend or relative of the customer, a window washer outside the salon, or someone who comes to rob the cashier! You can do this exercise, each writing a different story, using all sorts of places: An amusement park, a beach, a college dorm, a restaurant, an airport....

*(Work in your notebook)*

Have each person **invent a past life for a pet**. This is fun in a group since often you know each other's pets. Was your cat a prospector during the Gold Rush? A French goat farmer? Was your dog a Russian cellist? A Greek botanist? A British jewel smuggler?

*(Work in your notebook)*

Is it someone's **birthday**? Have each person in the room write a story that places everyone in the group in an unusual location for a party, as the birthday girl or boy enters, riding on a ---- (you decide!) and describe what happens.

*"Make it a snake and you'll live to regret it!"*

*"Nardo, don't be a big shot. You're not a real snake anyway."*

*"Oh, yeah? Take THIS!"*

*"That tickles. Your tongue is red felt."*

*"I can turn it into flame!"*

*"Sure, you can."*

*(Work in your notebook)*

Have each person in the group make a "Coming Attractions"

poster for the soon to be released **movie version** of one of your stories. Is it a horror version of a sweet story? A scary movie based on a scary story? Is it animated or live action? Make up the names of the actors, or use famous ones. Be sure to write what the movie studio would put on the poster to get people to come see the film.

**DESIGN YOUR MOVIE POSTERS** *in your notebook.*

**CREATIVE FIELD TRIPS**

Go to a **cemetery**. Place tissue paper over the name and dates of birth and death on someone's gravestone, then rub with a crayon to make yourself a copy. **Now, invent your character's life story.**

*(Work in your notebook)*

Observe people in a **shopping mall**, and choose which one is a **mind reader or a spy**. Write the biography of your "character" then put him or her in a story.

*(Work in your notebook)*

**DREAMS, SENSES AND MEMORIES**

Your **dreams** at night and daydreams can bring you ideas for stories, and can be used in stories, but ending a story with "And it was only a dream!" hasn't worked well since "The Wizard of Oz". Too many writers who don't know how to end their stories well just use the dream excuse. Yes, it's a nice change from "And everyone died" but you can do better.

Think of a **dream you've had**, and use any part of it to inspire a story. There are probably lots of interesting dreams you remember, so come back to this exercise as you work through the book.

Try using dreams another way. A character can dream about a robbery, and during the dream he really is robbed. Does the real thief steal what the victim dreamed about? Is the thief the same one as the one in the dream? What if someone steals from the thief? Or it's the thief who's dreaming about being robbed? What if the thief only steals an idea from him, instead? Try an original story that combines dreams and burglary.

*(Work in your notebook)*

Most people have had an **absurd dream** about showing up for class in their underwear, or having completely forgotten to study for a big test. Write about such an experience, and make it seem as realistic as you can. Is the character in his or her underwear embarrassed, or surprisingly relaxed? Do people snigger, or pretend not to notice? Are the teachers laughing or mad? You can make the outcome anything you'd like!

*(Work in your notebook)*

Write about a dream and a character not having the dream, but perhaps in the dream. See what it's like to go from reality to the dream, as you advance your story.

*(Work in your notebook)*

**"What if Nardo was just a dream?"**

**"In your dreams!"**

Write about someone who writes while sleeping. Does she do so sleepwalking, or is she **dreaming she's writing**? What if she could only write when she was asleep? Would he remember everything once he woke up? Would she finish her story, and if so, while she was awake or while she was asleep? What if she fell asleep afterwards and never woke up to show it to anyone?

*(Work in your notebook)*

Try to remember the most **unusual dream** you've ever had, and then make it into a story. You can add any part missing from the dream, so that your story flows well. If you can't think of a dream strange enough, then try to remember one in which something didn't work. This is a classic dream, too. You're pouring water and it keeps spilling, you open the toothpaste tube and toothpaste squishes everywhere, you try to talk, but you have so much gum in your mouth, no words come out...

*(Work in your notebook)*

You can also let a portion of a perfectly **average dream** inspire a story. Maybe it was a chair in the dream, that reminds you of your grandparents, or the way a breeze blew some curtains, that brings vacations to mind. Take any part of a "normal" dream, and use it to build a story.

*(Work in your notebook)*

What's the **first thing you can remember** about being little? If it's a crib with bars, you're not alone. But maybe there's another specific memory from later on in those early years. What do you remember understanding back then? Did you ever know what you wanted to say without having the vocabulary to say it?

*(Work in your notebook)*

Now take that or another early memory and describing it focusing on **two senses**, perhaps sight and sound or taste and smell. Imagine how an infant with limited experience in the world might give enormous importance to details.

*(Work in your notebook)*

**SENSE YOUR SENSES**

Think of a **scent** that makes you feel safe and loved. Your grandmother's soap? Your father's aftershave? Now, a **touch** that leaves you feeling the same way. A brother's arm around your shoulders? Holding your mother's hand? Next, find a **taste** that's as comforting. For some, it might be seeded rye bread and sweet butter, for others, pumpkin pie. Now, find a comforting **sound**. A child shuffling down a hallway in slipper socks? Your dog's sigh as he sleeps? Add a comforting **sight**. Is it the porch light on at night? Or your sister's hoodie, under her house keys? Each person's senses are stirred by different things. Write about a few of your important **sensory memories.**

*(Work in your notebook)*

**Remember** the time before you knew how to swim or knit, fry an egg or ride a bike. Did you watch people who could and think they had magical powers? Did it seem as if your hands and feet would never work the way theirs did? Chronicle the stages of before, during and after you learned how. Write what it felt like and how it feels to be able to do it now, without even thinking about it. Do little kids watch you now and think you have magical powers?

*(Work in your notebook)*

Senses can be overwhelmed to leave a character completely out of balance, or **discombobulated**. He might drink, but only gets thirstier, eat, but just get thinner. The more he washes, the more he might smell. Hair can appear messier after it's combed, and, if one is stuck somewhere, the later it gets, the more time can appear to stand still. Write about **sensory overload**, when the usually remedy only makes things worse.

*(Work in your notebook)*

This next exercise takes **senses** and displaces them. Instead of seeing a sight, hearing a sound, and smelling a scent, the verbs and nouns interchange. So now, you'd hear a flower's perfume or taste pollution in the sky. What other noises can you imagine seeing? What sort of sights could you feel? What kind of scents could you hear? Experiment with **displacing your senses**. You're bound to come up with something very interesting.

Admittedly, this one is difficult....

*"THEN I'M NOT DOING IT."*

*"Hush, Nardo. This is an exercise in which you mix the senses. You can speak a taste, see a sound or hear a sight. If you write 'The fluorescent orange and pink bathing suit screamed to everyone on the beach', that's a sight you can hear. If you write: 'The thunder pounded the grey clouds to a pulp', that's a sound you can see. Come up with as many as you can."*

*"I VOTE FOR NONE!"*

*"Okay, final score: Nardo zero. Writing students: Way, way more."*

How many examples of mixed sense can you describe? Try seeing a taste, touching a sound, hearing a sight... Here's one to get you started: **Write about the "sound of purple"**.

*(Work in your notebook)*

# CHAPTER 5:

# HARVEST YOUR HYBRIDS

There are even more ways to think creatively when you write and draw. In this chapter, you'll **mix all sorts of ideas**, then find some unusual ways of working with **poetry**.

Choose a **character** from **any book** and put him or her into the **setting** in **any film**. The film can be live action or animated. (It doesn't matter if the film was based on a book.) What if Harriet the Spy finds herself in the crowd from "Aladdin" during the parade for Prince Ali, or Percy Jackson ends up in "Cloudy With a Chance of Meatballs" and be hit in the head with a slice of pie? You can introduce the character without changing the plot of the film. How does she or he react to the setting? Find another example and then **write and illustrate the scene in which your character discovers the new setting.**

*(Work in your notebook)*

You can also **mix two movies**, putting **characters** from either into the other movie's **plot**. What if the opossum from "Over the Hedge" took a trip with the saber tooth tiger from "Ice Age"? What if Violet from "The Incredibles" and Penny from "Bolt" were roommates in college? What if the Prince from "enchanted" was best friends with Shrek? This time, you'll change the plot of the movie to accommodate the new character. Now, mix characters from **two books**, and feel free to change to plot. Maybe Milo from "The Phantom Tollbooth" meets Ariel from "The Little Mermaid", Anne of Green Gables and Piglet have a picnic with Tigger, or Alex Rider asks Sammy Keyes on a date.

*(Work in your notebook)*

Here's a fun one for your senses: Describe participating in a **pie eating contest**. What kind of pie is it? Do you get apples up your nose? Custard in your eyes? Peaches in your ears? Does is squish or crunch? Is the crowd cheering or throwing plastic spoons? Describe every sight, sound, texture, taste and aroma.

*(Work in your notebook)*

Now, a real challenge: Describe **something you've never experienced**, imaging how it would feel. Here's your chance to scuba dive, perform a kidney transplant or conduct a symphony orchestra.

## HAIKU AND POETRY

**Haiku** is a form of poetry that originated in Japan, most often with 5 syllables in the first line, 7 in the second line, and 5 in the third line. Because it's so confined, haiku is an ideal format for exploring **one emotion** at a time. Pain, loneliness, anger, jealousy, love, sadness, elation and frustration all work well. You can also consider single notions such as genius, surprise, incomprehension, kindness, rejection or silliness. You may also try of these descriptions by writing a poem, instead, without counting syllables. Which do you like better?

A haiku can reconcile **two opposing ideas**:

Bumbling and stumbling

I'm forever tumbling down....

Time now to stand up.

See how the ideas of **up and down** are introduced? The down is preceded by so many words, it feels as if you're falling down the stairs. The up is at the end, alone, in the clear for a new start. Write some haiku using opposing ideas, such as silence and noise, high and low, light and dark.

*(Work in your notebook)*

Like all poetry, haiku can use **alliteration**, a series of words beginning with the same letter:

Slimy snails slinking

Shells crunching under my shoe

Sticky messy floor


You can also repeat words:

Clunky clumps: Copper keys

Clack clack clatter clumsily

Casual crashes


Write two haikus about the same subject, making **one positive and one negative**. You could write about a lovely flowering tree in one haiku, and a spooky, dead stump in the next one. Or, describe a princess who is physically beautiful in one haiku, and horribly mean and dishonest in the second one.

*(Work in your notebook)*

You can also use haiku to write an **ode**, which is a romantic salute to someone or something:

Oh, best and brightest

Exploding with ideas

Stars of the 5th grade

Or:

Hail the cunning brain

Crafting words in middle age

Burn, creative fire!


Soon, you'll write an **ode to a hated vegetable**, so start thinking about which one you'll choose. Of course, you adore every single vegetable, and given your way, that's all you'd ever eat, so you'll just have to pretend you don't like one. Pickled turnips or sweet and sour endives, perhaps?

*(Work in your notebook)*

Now, write an ode to an item of **clothing you dislike**, using lots of lavish praise and extremes. You'll be "romancing" this item you passionately can't stand.

*(Work in your notebook)*

Write a haiku for any of the **seasons** and avoid the obvious: flowers in spring, snow in winter, heat in summer and falling leaves in autumn. Instead, try to cite the most unusual thing about that season. What about melted ice cream or the smell of tar in summer, rotting gourds and less sunlight for fall, slipping on ice or having hot chocolate burn your tongue in winter and bugs flying in your face, or too many earthworms in spring?

*"Not to overly focus on what's negative...."*

*"Not at all, Nardo. Some of Cathy's best friends are worms."*

*(Work in your notebook)*

It's always interesting to take a poem somewhere **unexpected**. Try finding a wonderful side of something that's bad. Maybe being sick in bed provides you with precious, quiet time, in which you make great plans.

Work on a poem about the **good side of a bad thing, or the bad side of a good thing**. "Beautiful Boredom", "Ode to Garbage", "The Squish of the Hug" or anything you invent.

*(Work in your notebook)*

Use **metaphors** and **similes** to describe a person in an original way. She had a heart as warm as a baked potato, he was as sweet as a rotting casaba melon, she was as cold as frost in a junk yard, they were as stiff as charred chips of driftwood, his anger was as red as a bleeding raspberry...

*(Work in your notebook)*

*"Cathy skipped 'Sneaky, soaring, snaky sight, gave a writer quite a fright."*

*"Nardo rhymed. But that provides an idea for another assignment: Write about a character who interrupts constantly. He can be---"*

*"What makes you so sure it's a 'he'?"*

*"Nardo, you're interrupting."*

**RHYMING**

You should realize by now that poetry need not rhyme to be good. Just let the words flow and see what you get. If you do like rhyming words, then work on using unusual ones. One student rhymed "orange" with "door hinge". You might add "spore tinge" "gore twinge" "lore binge" and "core singe". You can rhyme the name Eunice with the descriptor "croonstress" which puts "crooner", a singer, in the feminine. (It shouldn't matter if it's not in the dictionary). Or rhyme "spaghetti" with "already". It's close enough. Just start with **a word you don't usually rhyme** and start playing with different sounds.

**SQUARE POEMS AND SHAPE POEMS**

The most famous Square Poem was written by Lewis Carroll. It's six lines of six words that read the same horizontally or vertically. They even make sense. Look it up, it's amazing! A more common assignment for kids is a **shape poem,** in which you write words that relate to the shape you've made, in that shape. For example, you draw a cat's head and write a poem about a cat. But this book is dedicated to what's uncommon, so you'll twist that exercise.

**DRAW AN OBJECT OR ANIMAL AND WRITE A POEM ALONG THE EDGES OR INSIDE THE SHAPE THAT HAS *NOTHING* TO DO WITH THE OBJECT OR ANIMAL.**

You can draw a hammer and write about daffodils, or draw a lemur and write about a rutabaga.

You may have had an assignment at school in which the teacher asks you to **take an emotion and decide what color it is.** Anger is usually red or black, happiness is pink or yellow, sadness is black or blue....

Now, be a rebel: Start with an emotion and give it the most surprising color you can. Some "wrong" colors could be: blue for anger, red for peace, yellow for jealousy or grey for happiness.

Write a short description of or a poem about how that color could work for that emotion. *"Anger is green/I feel so obscene."* It doesn't have to rhyme. You may decide to describe anger is yellow: *"My anger was bright and sharp, like yellow lightning."* See how you make it make sense, in a way no one else could.

*(Work in your notebook)*

Take a famous poem, **keep the rhythm and change the words**. This exercise helps you see how well your words fit a given rhythm. The two poems used below are among Cathy's favorites ever written. Look up the original words and read them aloud, for a real treat.

*"Annabelle Lee" by Edgar Alan Poe*

*It was penny and penny, I tossed into a big jar made of clay*

*That made the sum to buy a shawl of the softest, warmest grey*

*And the woman that wore it glowed with pride on that frigid, wintry day...*

*Or, "Where the Sidewalk Ends" by Shel Silverstein*

*There is a face where the eyebrows bend*

*Far above a ski-jump nose....*

Of course, you know reading is good for your writing and thinking, thinking is good for your reading and writing, and writing is—

**"They get it, boss. Enough."**

**"Okay. Sorry, Nard."**

Write some poems using gerunds: swirling, falling, sparkling....It's interesting to play with the repeated "ing" sound. See what you come up with.

*(Work in your notebook)*

**All alliteration**. Choose a letter of the alphabet and write a paragraph using only words which start with that letter. See how surprising your sentences can be.

*Ulla uttered "Ugly umbrella" understandably.*

You can also write a poem or haiku this way. (Remember a haiku has 5 syllables in the first line, 7 syllables in the second line and 5 syllables in the third.)

*Hating haiku here*

*Hasty, hurried. Hardly heard/Happy?*

*Hog heaven!*

*(Work in your notebook)*

## CONCEPTS THAT CATAPULT

Looking for more subjects for a poem? Try circles and cycles, transformations, confusion, time, sleeping, justice or just being alive.

*(Work in your notebook)*

Try assigning **colors** to nouns that have none, such as "laziness", "greatness", "memory", "accuracy", "goodness" or "wanderlust". The choices are not obvious, but will get you thinking.

*(Work in your notebook)*

Choose other nouns and use **original descriptors** of them is a series of poems. How would a "heart like a butterfly" differ from a "heart like sour cream"? How would the "courage of a slab of concrete" compare to the "courage of a snowflake"?

*(Work in your notebook)*

Make **traditions untraditional.** Instead of writing about the usual reasons you love your parents on Mother's or Father's Day, compose a poem about something that makes them original. Maybe your dad tends to sneeze three times in a row, or your mom can never remember the words to a certain song.

*(Work in your notebook)*

In every class, there's a student who yearns to change the assignment. Write a poem about a **changed creative work,** whether it's because you wanted to change it, someone made a change after you'd completed working, or that the assignment was changed, just as you'd figured out what you'd create.

**HOLD A BAD WRITING FESTIVAL**

Just in time, in case you weren't pleased with your poetry! Here's a chance for you to enjoy writing some really terrible stuff, forgive yourself and move on.

*"Why 'move on', when they can STAY as uncreative as possible forever?"*

*"If we have Snake Charming Festival, or a Charming Snake Festival, you'll be notified."*

Describe some characters using too many **cliché adjectives**. *"Her tousled, silky mane"* instead of *"her hair"*. *"Her lithe, lovely limbs"* instead of *"her legs"*. Award the worst example.

*(Work in your notebook)*

Write the **worst poem** you've ever seen or heard. Make sure the words look and sound awful.

*(Work in your notebook)*

Write a story about writing the **worst story ever**, and winning the bad writing contest. But describe the process of writing it and the feelings about it so well that it becomes a **good** story! Aha! You knew Cathy would get you back on track, didn't you?

*(Work in your notebook)*

Now, after you've done all this and laughed, go back and find a way to make that bad story even **more interesting**. Then, get rid of the clichés and rewrite the character descriptions so they're unexpected and **compelling**. Keep the poem lousy, though. Just kidding! Find a way to bring out the **uniqueness of the poem**. Reread all your bad writing entries and give them a polish (that means change some words) so they get better.

*(Work in your notebook)*

If you can do all this, you've not only rescued some bad writing from the trash, you're well on your way to becoming an artist.

## MUSIC

Write a poem about a **color** and give it a tune. Figure out harmonies and favor the unexpected: What if light green is sung on a low note and dark grey is sung on a high one?

*(Work in your notebook)*

Now, give colors to different musical **instruments**. Make your choices surprising. A bass could be pink and a flute could be black. Write a poem using the sounds and colors.

**Change the lyrics and keep the tune**. You've all heard *"Happy birthday to you, you belong in a zoo..."* The funniest songs with changed lyrics tend to contrast the subject or the tone with the original song. "Michelle" by The Beatles could go *"Michelle, you smell, Like a rose between two dirty toes. I hold my nose..."*

*(Work in your notebook)*

You don't have to keep the same subject. **A sweet tune can have ghoulish lyrics** and vice versa. Mary Had a Little Lamb can have these words *"Vampire Jethro's stalking you"*. Nothing too scary, please!

Try a few **new lyrics** yourself, this time, using a serious or scary tune and inventing babyish, nursery rhyme lyrics for it. You can take Beethoven's Fifth Symphony, and sing *"My blankie now!"....*

*(Work in your notebook)*

If you're not a singer, try working with **sounds.** Write a story that includes **one sound of a living thing** (a baby crying, a donkey braying, a person humming, a seal barking...) and **one sound of**

**a non-living thing** (a door slamming, a tea kettle whistling, an elevator dinging, an iron steaming…)

*(Work in your notebook)*

Now, write about the **"Heard Word"** whether it's spoken or sung, rhymes or not. Every day, you hear songs, announcers and conversations. Sometimes the message is serious, sometimes it's foolish. What word have you heard?

*(Work in your notebook)*

Another non-musical music prompt is **"Take Note"**. Is your character taking notes by writing on a page during a meeting or class, or is he or she appropriating musical notes to use in his writing? What role will "take note" have in your story, and what characters will you invent?

*(Work in your notebook)*

Even if you've never rapped, you can probably reproduce the rhythm rappers use. Try rapping about unusual things, like erasers, shoelaces or washcloths.

*"My pen won't work. It leaks, what a mess. I feel like a slob with ink on my dress."* Choose any subject and write a **rap**.

*(Work in your notebook)*

Write a poem using the words for **notes**: Do, re, mi, fa, so, la and ti, as well as their **homonyms** doe, ray, me, so and tea. It may take some effort to not think about Julie Andrews in "The Sound of Music". Choosing a different meter and a subject other than music will help:

*Rémi, my flea,*

*So hard to see,*

*Slurps noisily*

*His scorching tea*

*(Work in your notebook)*

Write a **lullaby to a turtle**. You can make up the tune, or use a standard lullaby tune, but make sure the words are original.

*(Work in your notebook)*

Write about two **neighbors who each play an instrument** of your choice. Describe the first time they meet. Do they live in houses or in an apartment building? How old are they? Have they been able to hear each other's music? Is each aware the other is a musician? Is one more accomplished than the other? Will they like each other?

*(Work in your notebook)*

Write about any **noise that bothers you**, musical or not. An electric saw? Grinding gears? How about a noise that bothers others, but not you? The squeak of your hamster's wheel? Now, write about a **non-musical noise you like**? The hum of a subway train?

*(Work in your notebook)*

Now write **"The Song You Don't Know"** and be sure to sing it with feeling. Tricky, isn't it?

*(Work in your notebook)*

Write a song for a musical comedy that takes place in a **Post Office.** It can be sung by customers or people who work there. Design a **poster** to advertise your musical.

*(Work in your notebook)*

Part of listening to music is noticing the pauses, or **silent beats.
Write a poem or story about the absence of sound.**

Cathy wrote this haiku:

*Every other note*

*Listen to what's in between:*

*The sound of nothing*

*(Work in your notebook)*

Write the **National Anthem of Taravina.** If you worked in a
group on the Taravina assignment, you can each write one line of
the anthem, based on something from your descriptions of the
country. Or, each of you can write an anthem and sing it for the
group. The refrain used in the workshop was "Taravina, Taravina.
It really is a place!"

*(Work in your notebook)*

# CHAPTER 6:

## REPOT YOUR PLOT
## AND BEWARE OF SNAKES

So far, you've seen that a certain amount of planning or rational editing balanced with unbridled joy results in pretty **great writing**. You have some more work to do, so put away your kazoos and tambourines for a minute. Time to get serious. (Don't worry, it won't last too long.)

**CHANGE THE PLOT**

These next exercises require looking at entire stories, then **redirecting part of their plots while keeping the characters intact.** Sometimes, the order of scenes will change, and sometimes, the settings will change. It's up to you to introduce new ideas and then hold these stories together.

**The set-up**: What if Little Red Riding Hood couldn't stand her grandmother so never packs the basket of goodies for her? Find a different start to this story, and decide where it goes. Does she walk through the woods anyway? Does she meet a wolf? Were they already friends?

**The middle**: What if Dorothy landed in a much different place than Oz? She could have a cat named Blubby Poo instead of a dog named Toto. Have her meet completely different friends in this new adventure, or keep characters from the original story, and take them on another journey.

**The end**: What if the Giant caught Jack instead of escaping? Would his mother get worried, climb up the beanstalk and save the day? Would she drag Jack home and move to Maplewood, NJ?

Experiment by changing the beginnings, middles and ends of other stories.

*(Work in your notebook)*

One way to get a sense of balance in your story is by charting it on a **number line**. This lets you examine the sequence of events, or "plot points'" horizontally, with the middle of your story at the midpoint. It can be hard to do this using vertical outlines since some events often end up off the page.

## STORY ON A NUMBER LINE

Consider **"Goldilocks"**:

**bears leave; girl breaks in; eats their food; breaks their chair; they return, upset; she runs away, scared**

This is the story in broad strokes, or main events. You could even make a graph of "Goldilocks with happy events plotted higher and sad events plotted lower. Connecting the events with straight lines may give you something that looks like a sales chart, but it will give you a sense of the pace and the climax of the story.

GOOD

NEUTRAL  **bears leave**

BAD  **girl breaks in... later, runs away, scared**

WORSE  **eats their food (disapproving of most of it), breaks their chair, tests their beds. The bears return, upset to see their home was invaded**

Is "Goldilocks" overall positive, negative, or do good and bad have equal time? Pretty negative, isn't it? You almost wish she'd apologize before running away. That would be nicer!

Now, consider what you could alter to make an original story. Not only can you change the character, plot and setting, you can change **TIME.** "Goldilocks" who may now be an ostrich, an old man or a 747, and can spend most of the story on the doorstep, deliberating about whether breaking in is a good idea or not. The bears could be a family of iguanas who live in Outer Mongolia.

**REWRITE GOLDILOCKS**

Fairy tales are short and simple, so make good examples, but it's better if you invent an entirely new story.

**CHART YOUR ORIGINAL STORY ON A NUMBER LINE, then write and illustrate your story**

Using a number line can also help you when you **edit**, since you keep an overview of the whole story. Once you change an event, it's easier to see how it will affect the other plot points.

**CHANGE ONE EVENT IN YOUR STORY** on your number line (or graph), then write your new story. You can illustrate anything that resulted from the change, as well.

*(Work in your notebook)*

How did the change you made effect the rest of your story? Is it
sadder, happier or the same, only moving in a different direction?
You may like one version more than the other, or like them
equally. You're really producing lots of creative work!!! Now for
some more relaxing exercises.

***Cathy just opened the door and discovered two dozen white
roses, real ones, arranged in a wicker basket with a note that
reads "U R mii wroze." O heart aflutter! This made her day!***

**While she's singing to herself and braiding ribbons into her
hair, please finish and illustrate this story:**

*Bebop was a 10 year old boy who walked everywhere with a
joyous bounce in his step, as if he had his own theme music
pulsing in his bones. He lived with a poor "aunt" who wasn't
really related to Bebop, but had decided to adopt him when he
was found as a baby in front of the Pottle Barber Shop. Everyone
in the town liked him, which can happen if, like Bebop, you
concentrate on your own life and don't really care who's
watching.*

*One day, as he pranced home from school, he found a strange
little box. He looked around to see who had dropped it, but no
one was there. He sat on a bench and looked at it.*

*A squirrel came up to him, and said, "I think you should open it."
Bebop replied, "You can talk?" The squirrel said "That's not the
point" and ran up a tree. Bebop wished they had spoken longer,
and decided to------------------*

*(Work in your notebook)*

Now write the beginning and the end to this **middle:**
**Your character is getting tired swimming and feels as if he or
she has been born swimming and will never stop for the rest
of his or her life.**

Where is your character swimming? A lake, pool or ocean? How long has he or she been swimming? Why?

*(Work in your notebook)*

Okay, since you really expect it, here's an **end** of a story. Up to you to write the beginning and the middle:

*"Hannah shook her head. She would not go back, not ever. She swung her bag onto her shoulder, and started down the long road."*

*(Work in your notebook)*

## MORALS

It can be interesting to write different morals for the same story. If you have your know-it-all who character become humbled just as your insecure character realizes he knows more than he thought, what could the moral of the story be? "Life is nicer when you learn something." "Everyone has some wisdom deep down" and "Have faith in yourself, but not too much!" all work. **Try finding morals** for stories you've written so far.

*(Work in your notebook)*

You can also start with a saying or motto, and **let that inspire a story**. Here are a few mottos to ponder: "You meet the same people on your way up as you do on your way down", "If at first you don't succeed, try, try again", "Take an umbrella, it never rains" or "Neither a borrower nor a lender be." You can also hijack these mottos to make them more original: "If at first you don't succeed, go live on a deserted island."

*(Work in your notebook)*

Imagine a world where **animals are in charge** and people are their pets. Might you belong to a gerbil, a crow, a Great Dane, a lizard, an elephant, a dolphin? What would life be like?

*"Probably a lot like living in someone's guts."*

*"You can always move, Nardo."*

*"But I just got new curtains!"*

Now, try a story where you're an animal's pet.

*(Work in your notebook)*

## ART

Write a story using the figures or shapes in a **painting** or on a vase at a museum. If it's abstract art, then invent a character or a setting from the forms you see. Then, choose someone in the museum who isn't looking at the art, and put that character in your story, as well. Is it a tired teacher? A janitor? A security guard? A bored parent with a kid who loves museums?

*(Work in your notebook)*

Open an art book to any page with a picture, and invent the name and **life history** of a character you choose. Try to avoid the obvious. Instead, make their thoughts and relationships refreshingly different from what you'd expect. If the picture doesn't include people or animals, then use the **setting** for an original story. Remember to make the events unexpected.

*(Work in your notebook)*

In the same way you'd make a collage, gluing bits of images to a paper, write a **"soundscape"** that includes bits of conversations. Imagine walking through an airport, train station, amusement park or a shopping mall and passing groups of people. You'd catch parts of what they say, but not all. In sequence, these bits generally won't make sense, but overall, they can form a piece that seems whole.

*Write your soundscape in your notebook*

Choose any strong feeling or emotion: love, hate, jealousy, exhilaration, frustration, happiness, anger, hope, despair, joy, exhaustion, fury, and write a list of materials you'd use to make a **collage of that emotion**. It's okay if this seems random, since it's a poetic assignment. To make a collage of exhilaration, you might use a light, metal spring that boings off the page, the scent of lemon rinds and fresh cut grass, heartbeats and the high notes on a flute. Your turn:

*(Work in your notebook)*

Another poetic assignment with words: Choose a **texture,** then write a poem describing it. Now, use art supplies to give the words different colors and textures, and glue what you make to your paper. The words don't have to be lined up neatly, in fact, they may appear to be flying across the page! What if the colors are not the obvious ones that match the words?

*(Work in your notebook)*

Invent then write about a new kind of **cuckoo clock**, with something other than a bird that pops out. Does the item come out on the hour, or at different times?

*Draw your clock in your notebook*

You had a poetry assignment choosing the **"wrong color"** for an emotion, then presenting a logic around it, so others can understand your choice. Now, make a **drawing** with all the "wrong" colors. The grass can be red, the sky can be green and the sun, purple. To make things even more interesting, write a **story** this inspires.

*(Work in your notebook)*

Here's one of the most difficult exercises in this book. Assign different colors to different **movements**. Standing up, sitting down, breathing in and out, running, jumping, as well as movements of mechanical objects or other inanimate objects blown by the wind or falling to the ground. Decide what happens to the colors during the movement. Do they burst, trickle or flicker? Do the colors have a volume or produce any sounds? Write a description or poem about these colored movements, then make a drawing or collage to go with it.

*(Work in your notebook)*

Now, choose two colors and describe a **three course meal** in which everything served is one of those colors. Think about what would taste good and what would look pretty but taste ghastly. You can make some of the meal delicious and some awful. Up to you.

*(Work in your notebook)*

With enough artistry, you can **find beauty in anything**. Write about the beauty of something that's not beautiful. A wart, bunion, scab, toad or manatee.

*(Work in your notebook)*

Assign a **color to any day of the week**, and explain your choice. Then decorate the letters of the word using that color scheme. Is Thursday maroon? Is Saturday silver?

*(Work in your notebook)*

Here's a chance to use your imagination as a photographer. Write about a character that finds a roll of undeveloped film (it still exists!) and takes it to a photo lab. Now, **describe the pictures** that someone had taken before losing the film roll.

*(Work in your notebook)*

## TIMED DRAWINGS.....AND WRITING

Now for a drawing exercise that can help you with your writing. Set some objects on a table and give yourself **three minutes** to draw them. Use anything; a pencil sharpener, an apple, a book, a comb. A still life need not be flowers in a vase.

**Draw your 3 minute still life.**

It's not a long time, but you'll find you make the most important lines first. The "broad strokes". You can do the same thing when you write, creating a character in three minutes, or describing the setting in three minutes.

**Write a 3 minute character or setting description:**

Now try a **whole story in ten minutes**. It can be able anything. Pace yourself, so you don't spend all your time on the opening paragraph or get stuck in the middle. Don't worry how well it turns out, just go for it, include what's most important to the beginning, middle and end, then race to the finish.

**Write your 10 minute story:**

Having a time limit can help you concentrate on the creative work and forget about your internal censor.

*"I don't like being ignored."*

*"Then be more encouraging."*

*"No can do."*

*"Come on, Nardo. Try to smile."*

*"Brace yourself."*

*"That's a leer. And you're hissing!"*

Draw your discouraging creature attempting to be supportive of you.

*(Work in your notebook)*

## DANCE BREAK!

If you're finding there too many of the same type of exercises in a row, then you're not **skipping around** enough in this book! Time to shake up your senses and get your ideas circulating again. This can be achieved by: standing on your head, doing jumping jacks, doing the Hokey Pokey (you can pretend you forgot how, but Cathy thinks you both know the truth). Put on some music, and you can lip synch to an Abba song. You'll get back to writing refreshed!

*Cathy just received her credit card bill. Nardo not only charged her for the flowers, he ordered a deluxe leather hammock from Abercrombie and Fitch, and subscribed to "Popular Fisherman" Magazine. As if he has time to go fishing when he has a novel to finish! Enough's enough. When he wakes up, he's out of here for good.*

Write an **argument** between two characters from each of their POVs, and then have a third character who observes the fight tell it from her or his POV. Maybe a friend borrowed your favorite shirt and lost it. Or maybe you witnessed someone copying during a test from someone who pretended not to notice.

*(Work in your notebook)*

Now, what if the argument were between you and your **sore arm**? Or between a piano and the person playing it?

*(Work in your notebook)*

Write from the POV of a character very **different** from you: a toothbrush, a racehorse, a dollar bill, a newborn baby, a spider. Try to put as much "humanity" as possible into this character. What does a racehorse think? What does a dollar feel? What does a spider wish?

*(Work in your notebook)*

Had enough of spiders? Now it's time to be a **fly on the wall**. The people in the room don't know this fly is listening to everything they say, watching everything they do, and will have his own take on the situation. Maybe he admires the people, maybe he mocks them. You decide.

*(Work in your notebook)*

Have you ever met someone who seemed **selfish** at first, but then becomes a nice friend? Or someone who seemed **nice** and then revealed him or herself to be a **creep** later? Tell the story of two such people you've known, even if you knew them at different times of your life, and describe when your opinion changed about each of them.

*(Work in your notebook)*

Choose a **bizarre disappearance** and describe it. Was your character ironing so long, he turned into vapor, or tickled so hard, she evaporated? Was he riding a rollercoaster that climbed so high, it vanished in the clouds? Try writing from the POV of the person who disappeared: Where did he or she go? Or, write from the POV of someone who witnesses the disappearance. Is he or she sad or glad to see the person go? This brings us to the next section.

*"Oh boy! Here comes my favorite!"*

*"That's a surprise, Nardo. We'd never have guessed. Is your suitcase packed? Then goodbye and good luck!"*

## REVENGE

There are times you feel so annoyed by something that happens, you can't help but think about revenge. Something unfair a teacher did or something mean a kid said will just stick in your mind and bother you. One way to feel better, fast, is to write a letter about it that you never send. It's pointless to spread anger around, so just **get it out of your system and then throw the paper away** so you can move on with your life.

*(Work in your notebook)*

Remember, it's more elegant to understate the crime rather than insult flat out. **Finesse your slander**. It's vastly more satisfying to appear to take the high road while cutting deep. Polite condescension where you appear gracious every second is the ticket.

Adults can write a letter that admonishes an aggravating boss or partner. Everyone remembers **a bad teacher**, they'd love to have fired. Try:

*"Dear Mr. Dipturfler, It has come to our attention that you've been forcing all your students to stand on one foot and face the wall for the entire Geography lesson...This may be a common practice on your home planet of Beznark, but it is hardly our style at Kippy Elementary. We hereby request you to take the same stance in front of the Board of Directors while we shred your contract and terminate your employment...."*

*"Terminate" indeed. Yes, Nardo was gone. Cathy took a bubble bath and met a friend for lunch. On the way home, she picked up a tin of expensive, spiced tea. This would be a time of careful attention to herself and to her writing. She felt tremendous!*

*Powerful! Free!*

*Two days later, she watched herself sobbing in the bathroom mirror. She hadn't written a sentence since he'd left. She felt empty, miserable and missed him so much, it made her crazy. She wrote him a note in lipstick on the medicine cabinet. "Cathy wuvs you. Come back." But he didn't. He was teaching her a lesson, which is fairly amazing for a character that isn't even real.*

Never lose sight of this excellent **African proverb**: "Sit peacefully on the riverbank. In time, you'll see all your enemies float by." It may take decades, but it works. Bad people do get theirs, so you can adopt a non-violent attitude and come out the winner. Over the long term, you can be satisfied knowing you're the nice one. But in the short term, it sure feels good to get back at someone mean by privately writing a story where **justice** is handed out. Remember, it's for your eyes only.

You can also write a poem to get **revenge**. Imagine that a bully named **Brefton Blobker** insulted you in the park. Try this out:

*If your earlobes stretched down to the floor,*

*And your sandwich got crushed by a boar*

*I'd want to sneer "eee-ew" whenever I'd see you*

*Instead, t'will be you I'll ignore*

Let off steam by inventing an apology written to you by someone who behaved badly. You can end it with a note back from you, saying "That's okay....(this time!)"

Here are a few more creative exercises to do that will leave you feeling even better:

Serenity is always better than anger, so try to imagine the **gentle disintegration** of your enemies. Dismantle them peacefully and systematically, as one would a bomb. Now write about then draw an enemy gradually falling apart.

*(Work in your notebook)*

Some negative things become positive when you write about them. People's failures and weaknesses can endear them to you. They make everyone seem more human. Write about a situation in which someone fails at something, but feels happier for having done so.

*(Work in your notebook)*

*A month has gone by. Cathy's written lots of revenge notes and torn them up, but hasn't done a lick of real work. This morning, standing in line for a coffee, the aroma of espresso caused a stir in her belly. Nardo was back, that rascal, and just waking up! No complaints or accusations, Cathy vowed. She'd behave as if she hadn't noticed his absence (Four weeks, two days, seven hours and twenty-two minutes)*

*"Oh, hi. Have a nice trip?"*

*No answer. It was now her turn to order.*

*"Ah ah ah I'd like ah ah ah latte, please" she said, through a hiccup attack.*

*Nardo was back, all right.*

Remember never to stoop to the level of the creeps you meet in life. It's a good trick to vent your anger in private, but keep it to yourself in public, so you're always more composed than those who bothered you! Onward and upward!

# CHAPTER 7:

## CHERISH YOUR GARDEN WORMS

This chapter presents yet more ways to spark creativity, while moving you to finish your projects.

**OBJECTS THAT INSPIRE**

"Swiss cheese, EKG, humming bird." To be honest, Cathy has no idea why she wrote this on her IDEAS page.

*"Nardo, did you write this down?" Oh, that's right. He wasn't here the past few weeks.... He'll speak up eventually. He always does. In the meantime, Cathy will concentrate on her work. If Nardo didn't make this note, let's assume she did.*

Could she have meant to list three unrelated things you could put into a story? Or did she think you'd find a relationship between the items? Tell you what. Make up a good exercise using these three things, and Cathy will publish the best one in her next book. For those of you who don't know, an EKG is a painless test they give to see how regularly your heart beats.

*"Mine beats only for Cathy."*

*"Hard to believe, after everything you've done." (Oh, he's back! He's back!!!! Isn't there a real heart sign on this keypad? <3 <3 <3 doesn't begin to convey the emotion!)*

*(Work in your notebook)*

List a few **random trios** of items you can use in a story, for example: a book, a hairbrush and a chicken. (Live or cooked. It can be a toy chicken, or a painting of a chicken, too). The three things need not have equal importance in your story, and need not be interrelated (the book can be a dictionary, not a cookbook with chicken recipes) but all three should be included in the story.

*(Work in your notebook)*

**Fruit** provides great writing prompts, since the taste can be remarkable, and the variety of textures make for detailed descriptions. Most everyone has had a memorable experience with fruit. Beyond slipping on a squished grape, a character can get a bit of apple skin caught between her teeth, or squirt grapefruit juice in his eye. She can savor a mango, then get all sticky. He can wince biting into a sour lime, but use it to make a delicious pie. And these are only real fruits. Think of all the times cough syrup was said to taste like cherries, or candy was "watermelon" flavored. Write about a fruit experience, and don't forget "sandy" apples and rotten strawberries.

*(Work in your notebook)*

Imagine a **scroll** with writing on it, found hidden away somewhere. Either write the story on the scroll, or write a story about who found it and where. Is it important or not? How?

Think of something you were either sad or glad about having **thrown away.** Write a few paragraphs about what the consequences were, if any.

*(Work in your notebook)*

Write a story about **a hat and a hard boiled egg**. What sort of hat is it and to whom does it belong? Does the egg get eaten?

*(Work in your notebook)*

Feel free to give your objects **feelings**. Imagine an impatient piece of furniture, a conceited doormat, an insecure painting, a jealous rock, an ambitious napkin or an angry cello.

*(Work in your notebook)*

Write a story about a **bone**. Is it in a living creature or sitting, dry in a science lab? Is it part of a sculpture? Is it a broken bone? A fish bone? A back bone? A bone through someone's nose in a far away land? A rubber dog bone?

*(Work in your notebook)*

Write a story about a **broken plate**. Was it cheap or valuable? Did it break before your story begins, during or after? Who ate from or eats from it? Is it one of those decorative plates you hang on the wall? Is it the dish your cat eats from?

***"It wasn't my fault. A sudden gust of wind swept it off the table."***

***"Nardo, the window's closed."***

*(Work in your notebook)*

Write about a **belt**. Is it leather or plastic? Cheap or expensive? Is it needed by the wearer, or is it just for decoration?

*(Work in your notebook)*

Write a story about **a heart and a clock**. Are they separate items, or will you have a heart-shaped clock? Does the clock work, or not? How about the other ticker, the heart? What if the clock stopped working when the heart stopped beating, or vice versa. Could someone be the Keeper of the Clock? Would this be the owner of the heart?

*(Work in your notebook)*

Write a whole story about a whole **watermelon**. Does it get eaten, thrown away, painted by an artist? You can write from a person's point of view, from a watermelon seed's point of view, or from the POV of a fly that keeps landing on a juicy slice.

*(Work in your notebook)*

Write a story that includes a **black stocking**. Is it being worn on a leg, or is it in a drawer? Is it over a light bulb in lieu of a shade, or is it pulled over the face of a bank robber?

*(Work in your notebook)*

What could more insignificant than a **receipt** from the grocery store? You throw it away the minute you get home, right? But you can use it. Look as the items you bought, and let them suggest a character. Do detergent and bleach suggest the coach of the soccer team washing the uniforms before the final game of the season? Do olives, mushrooms and nuts make you imagine a mom from Jupiter buying dinner for her family? Or the owner of a bowling alley hosting a wedding reception? Maybe this receipt is the only clue a Police Detective has to finding a murderer? What's the story?

*(Work in your notebook)*

Chronicle the **strangest injury** ever. It can be a real one, or one you invent. One student was swimming in the Atlantic Ocean, and a jellyfish stung her armpit. Another student had an uncle who peed on an electrical fence, and got a shock! Yeowch! Another was cleaning apartments to make extra money, and singed her eyebrows off when a stove exploded. Write about another strange injury:

*(Work in your notebook)*

Can you picture the priceless **bronze statue in the Temple of Karthpashnu**? Neither can anyone else, since Cathy just made it up. Describe the statue, then put it in a story.

*(Work in your notebook)*

## A FEW MORE FOR A RAINY DAY

Is it really rainy? Where? Did it rain yesterday? Write a story about **weather.**

*(Work in your notebook)*

Who is **"The Keeper of the Combs"**? Develop this character and put him or her in a story. Other characters you can work on: **The Counter of Souls, The Princess of Misery, The Thought Poisoner, The Stacker of Time** or **The Designer of Paths.** (Thanks to Yasmine for coming up with the Princess of Misery)

Have you ever blown the fuzz off a **dandelion** stem, and watched it float away? Picture a breezy day, when the fuzz lands in a girl's hair. Who is this girl? She brushes it away, and it floats onto something else. Follow its path for the next few hours. Where does it go and what happens to it?

*(Work in your notebook)*

Where and what is **Club Kaleidoscope?** Write a detailed description, including the front door, decor and members.

*(Work in your notebook)*

Imagine an **animal that longs to be a musical instrument.** Describe which one and why?

*(Work in your notebook)*

Describe an **"un-birthday" party.** Could it take place on someone's birthday? Could it be set in a coal mine? Will guests have a good time or a terrible time? Make it as unexpected as you can.

*(Work in your notebook)*

**"The leather hammock I ordered was going to be your birthday present."**

*And by hogging it all day, Cathy supposes Nardo is breaking it in for her?*

In the spirit of experimentation, **change the purpose of each room** in your home. What if your bathroom becomes a closet, your living room becomes a bedroom, your kitchen turns into the room in which you bathe, or your bedroom becomes a laundry room? Describe what it feels like to live there for a day.

*(Work in your notebook)*

## SITUATIONS THAT SPARK STORIES

A character in a **motel room** hears noise in the next room through the thin walls. Had he seen who else checked in? Can he hear the occupants talking or is the noise from a TV, radio or musical instrument? Is it a celebration? Does it seem like a fight? Does your character take action by knocking on the wall or putting pillows over his ears? Where is this motel and what happens in the morning?

*(Work in your notebook)*

Your character takes a **job she hates** in a place she hates, for more money than she ever imagined. Describe the job, the character and what happens. Was it worth it, for the salary, or does she regret it?

*(Work in your notebook)*

*"I'm not signing until I get six weeks of vacation a year, Thursdays off and an exercise bike in my office."*

*"What job are you applying for, Nardo?"*

*"The ad didn't say, but I'm positive I can do anything."*

*"That's the ticket." Confident guy!*

Write a story about a character's journey via any mode of **transportation**: bike, train, bus, car, truck, caravan, kayak, canoe, walking, hitchhiking, swimming, running, sailing, power boat, plane, helicopter, hang-glider, unicycle, stilts, rickshaw, rocket, camel, skis, mule, llama….Who is your character? What is the destination and what happens along the way? **Draw the mode of transportation in your notebook**.

Imagine standing in the checkout line at a **grocery store**. Describe the person in front of you and what he or she is buying, then make suppositions about what the person is like, based on their purchases. You can also put the character in a story.

*(Work in your notebook)*

**Waiting** can inspire a story. A character might be at a doctor's office, movie theatre, clothing store, museum, school cafeteria, in line or not. He or she might be standing on a corner waiting for someone, or waiting indoors for someone to finish in the bathroom. Write a story in which a character is waiting for someone or something. Describe his or her mood and posture, and all the sensations involved. Is he slumping or standing straight? Is she cold or hungry? Does he have to go to the restroom? Is she happy or annoyed?

*(Work in your notebook)*

Imagine **sliding off your chair, under your desk and disappearing**. Where do you go and what happens?

*(Work in your notebook)*

Write an original story about **babysitting**, from any point of view. How do the kids behave? What if they're cooperative and the sitter is wild? How old is the sitter? Is it a regular sitting job, or is it the first time? You don't have to write an action-packed melee; it's possible nothing much happens. Who else could be in your story?

*(Work in your notebook)*

Five different characters are riding on a **bus that breaks down**. Where? On a city street, or a dirt road? On a highway in the middle of nowhere, or at the end of a pier, at the water's edge? Were they going to work and in a hurry, or is it late and dark outside? Are they on vacation? Do they have packages? Can any of them fix what broke? How do they interact and what happens? Try a sad ending as well as a happy one.

*(Work in your notebook)*

Your character **finds a suitcase.** Where? What's inside? Does he keep it a secret or tell someone else?

*(Work in your notebook)*

Write about a situation in which a character expects to feel one way, but instead feels completely different. Maybe he thinks he'll be sad when a close friend moves away, but unexpectedly, he feels free instead. Or, she thinks she'll be happy to attend her friend's party, then realizes she feels lonely. Write about **an unexpected reaction,** and surprise yourself.

*(Work in your notebook)*

Now, consider setting and character as you begin a story: You're travelling somewhere (Memphis? Monte Carlo? Madagascar? Are you going by bus, canoe, airplane, train or camel?) when suddenly, a **character you don't know** blocks your path. Who is it and what happens?

*(Work in your notebook)*

**Endings** can inspire great writing. Think about the end of a play, the school year, a friendship, a race, a ruler or a sandwich. Endings often give way to new beginnings: Leaving one place usually involves arriving somewhere else; changing means something else replaces what was. Write about an ending.

## CAN'T YOU BE MORE NEGATIVE?

*"I couldn't have said that better myself."*

*"That's why these next exercises are dedicated to you, Nardo."*

What is it that makes mistakes, disagreements, flaws and regrets so interesting? They're all part of being human. We recognize ourselves in these situations, and feel relieved when we're not at fault. Give the following a try, and feel like a good member of the human race.

Find a situation in which a character knows he or she is about to make an **error,** but is unable not to do so. He could be cutting fabric and knows he should stop and measure, but just keeps cutting, or she could be pouring juice into a pitcher, but simply unable to stop before it overflows. Is it from a lack of mental attention or a physical problem? Is it an action they dread, or does it satisfy an irresistible urge to cause trouble? You decide.

*(Work in your notebook)*

The above is an action that goes too far. Now, find a situation in which a character **says too much**, either blurting out a secret, over apologizing or making too many annoying jokes. The character doesn't have to be insensitive; sometimes, people who care very much overdo it.

*(Work in your notebook)*

Now, chronicle an argument in which both parties seem **wrong**. It can be about something important, or something insignificant. Other characters or a narrator might be useful to help the reader understand how each of the arguing characters are wrong. Are the additional characters friends or outsiders? Your story can be serious, comic or neutral in tone. Up to you.

*(Work in your notebook)*

Sometimes, a character **abruptly changes** his mind, for reasons that are sincere or not. He might change opinions to spare someone's feelings, or pretend to agree with an idea to seem more popular, or just feel outnumbered or ashamed, and go against his own judgment. Write about a character who suddenly changes his or her mind. How do the other characters react? Is the change of opinion peaceful or violent? Is it honest or false?

*(Work in your notebook)*

Write about a situation in which one character is **misunderstood**. This could happen because another character isn't very smart or because the first character is speaking gibberish. Will the one speaking try using different words or just say the same thing more clearly, or slower or louder? Where are your characters and how important is it that they be able to communicate?

*(Work in your notebook)*

Now, **describe a room in which an error occurred**. It can be any sort of mistake, and any type of room.

*(Work in your notebook)*

## EVERYBODY'S DOING IT

As you grow up, all sorts of fads come and go. Some people collect cards or objects. Other times, the trend involves something to wear. In this assignment, you'll **invent a fad**, describing how and where it started, how it caught on and when it all came to an end. One student proposed everyone would start wearing pig masks. Hilarious to imagine. Do you think it would ever catch on? Invent your trend:

*(Work in your notebook)*

Now, consider different rituals that exist in the world. There are Asian tea ceremonies, brushing your hair one hundred strokes before you go to bed or doing jumping jacks in the morning. There are ritualistic meals like Thanksgiving turkey with stuffing, bridal rituals of throwing the bouquet and sports fan rituals of doing "the wave" in the stadium after a homerun. **Invent a new ritual** and explain its meaning.

*(Work in your notebook)*

Write one of those annual **Christmas letters** some people send, but have the news be very odd and unexpected. Instead of: "The gang decorated the tree, then went for a sleigh ride while Grammy baked the gingerbread" you might have spent January making faces in front of the bathroom mirror, February seeing how long you could hold your breath and March learning to walk on your hands. The Christmas letter need not be sent in December, either.

*(Work in your notebook)*

Write about a character that can't help **laughing**, in a situation in which laughter is inappropriate. What are the thoughts in his or her head? How do others react? Try to choose a very original situation, and describe it fully (setting, weather, time of day).

*"Like the time Cathy was in the middle of coloring her hair and had to let in the meter reader?"*

*"That wasn't funny, Nardo. You're totally grounded, by the way."*

*(Nardo's really back! He's back, HE'S BACK!!!)*

*(Work in your notebook)*

### The Post-Vacation Lie

Making up what you didn't do over a school break can be even more refreshing than the week or two off. Stop at nothing while you invent and exaggerate what a character did over his or her vacation. Scale Mount Everest? Build an igloo? Corner the market on plutonium?

*(Work in your notebook)*

## DIARY ENTRIES

Take any character you worked on so far, living or inanimate, and imagine what he or she would write in a **diary** A) after moving to a new house, school or job B) after a fight with a friend, relative or boss C) after failing at something D) after discovering something wonderful.

Include feelings along with the facts. Are there things the character would write in a diary but not share with anyone aloud?

*(Work in your notebook)*

## NURSERY RHYMES

Sometimes, you learn **nursery rhymes** when you're so young, it's hard to fully understand the characters. Maybe you thought Humpty Dumpty was a hard boiled egg, and Jack and Jill were brother and sister, or fiancés? In any case, nursery rhyme characters are a good source for writing ideas.

Imagine Old King Cole wasn't so merry one day, or Jack and Jill had a fight halfway up the hill. What if Mother Hubbard found an original way to feed her dog, or the Old Woman who lived in the shoe managed to secure a nice apartment in Santa Monica? See what you can do with nursery rhyme characters and settings.

*(Work in your notebook)*

## BODY PARTS

If one day, you can't decide what to write about, remember that you yourself are inspiration for a story, from head to toe. Just choose a body part and watch a story take off.

Write a story about a **hand**. Is it a sculpted hand in a museum? A severed hand in a jar of formaldehyde? Is it in a glove? If it's someone's hand, whose is it? Snow White's? Frankenstein's?

*(Work in your notebook)*

Give your body parts even more personality. What would happen if you hand was mad at your foot? Write an **argument between you and your stomach**.

*(Work in your notebook)*

Write a story about a **belly button**. Is it in a painting, or on a beach? Does it belong to someone thin and pale or to someone fat and tan? Is it an "innie" or an "outie"? Can it talk?

*(Work in your notebook)*

Now, write about a **throat.** Does it belong to an announcer with laryngitis, a swan, a figure in a painting by Modigliani? Is it wrinkled, adorned with a necklace and/or being examined during an autopsy or is it vibrating during an aria at the Metropolitan

Opera?

*(Work in your notebook)*

Nothing gets kids more gleeful about writing than a butt-related subject. **Butts** are cheeky little creatures, but in Cathy's classes, they're kept spanking clean yet are still have lots of fun. Write about a butt from outer space, your old teacher's flat as a pancake butt, a baby's plump bottom, a wrinkled, skinny butt and an oversized butt. Invent a theme park called "Buttorama". What would the rides be like? (Do make sure to keep what you write polite, so people would want to go there!)

Write a story about an **eye**. Is it open, closed, crying, colored with make-up, seeing, swollen, in a photograph, or does it belong to a fish? Is the fish alive or dead? What if the eye of a dead creature could see?

*(Work in your notebook)*

Write a story about an **elbow**. Is it an elbow that shoved you in the subway, a cat's elbow, an animated frog's elbow, or part of a sculpture by Michelangelo?

*(Work in your notebook)*

Now write a story about a **tooth**. Is it loose, pointy, or in a perfect smile for a toothpaste ad? In the mouth of a giraffe, gopher or dinosaur? On a key ring? In a box of baby teeth? Has it been lost by a kid or an elderly person? Your story could involve counting a horse's teeth to tell his age, describe a root canal or concern a dentist in love.

*(Work in your notebook)*

What if your **hair** could talk and whispered thing into your ear that no one else could hear? Might it give you the answers during a test? Would you get caught and sent to the principal's office?

Might it whisper insults into other people's ears, who think you insulted them yourself? Could one hair get into a fight with one of your shoulders? How would you look as you walked down the street and told them to make less noise? This exercise was inspired by a student named Calypso.

*(Work in your notebook)*

## LANGUAGE

**Onomatopoeias** are words that sound like their meanings. Some examples are "crunch," "crack," "boing" and "zoom". Write a paragraph including some onomatopoeias you invent. If you're baking, you might write: *"I glooped some yogurt into the batter and blopped it around."* Your turn.

*(Work in your notebook)*

Take a character known for something and make a list of terms to describe him or her, using **gerunds,** the form of the verb that ends in "ing". For example, a farmer could be a *"seed planting, garden weeding, coop building, tractor driving, crop harvesting guy"* and a ballerina could be a *"plié doing, tutu wearing, chignon making, toe pointing, stage leaping, arm sweeping gal."*

*"I'm picturing an 'idea having, note taking, keyboard pounding, chocolate pudding for snakes depriving---"*

*"Nardo, finish your vegetables and we'll talk."*

**Idioms** are accepted expressions that don't always make sense. We say "that's another kettle of fish" to mean a different issue, "a little bird told me" to mean getting inside information and "kick the bucket" to mean die. Some are so overused, they weaken writing. Try inventing some new idoms and explain their uses:

*(Work in your notebook)*

Now, invent some new words to describe important or interesting

things which you think are missing in our language.
**"Heartmail"** could be when you send a letter to help mend a broken heart, something small and dear to you could be **"charmette"** something unappealing could be **"disgusterating"** while something terrific could be **"superlastic"**.

*(Work in your notebook)*

You can also mix the sounds of words, to invent new ones. At the end of the summer, are your sandals scuzzy, grungy or worse? Maybe they're **scrungy and gruzzy**. Make up some new descriptive words.

*(Work in your notebook)*

Now, combine even more words and invent ways to express feeling guilty, joyous, confused, defiant or slow. Could **"shameticious"** work for "guilt" and **"mentrifused"** mean "confused"? How does **"nagativity"** sound as the behavior of someone who continually discourages you?

*(Work in your notebook)*

Think of a **word** you don't like, because of its sound or meaning ("sludge"?), or a word with a sound you like, but a meaning you dislike. "Restriction" has a nice sound, but is not the most cheery word in the dictionary. You can also choose a word with a meaning you do like, but a sound you don't. "Booth" promises an intimate cubby hole, but may sound silly to some people. Now, write a spirited protest of what you don't like about the word you chose and why.

*(Work in your notebook)*

**WRONG? RIGHT!**

Find a sense for these phrases which use the **"wrong" words**: "deadening buds", "scorching snow", "euphoric despair" or "triumphant loss". Who says they can't mean something?

What other "wrong" words  might be interesting to describe **foods**? Imagine if bread could be "juicy" rice could be "squeaky" or nuts could be "sour." Invent some more and give them a meaning.

*(Work in your notebook)*

Now, find more "wrong" words to describe the sounds of musical instruments. Could a piano "roar", a piccolo "howl", a drum "coo" and a violin "baa"? Could you strum a flute or tickle a bass? What if a guitar could meow, a drum could moo and a bassoon could bark? Keep going, and put your strange instruments in a **poem you illustrate**.

*(Work in your notebook)*

After inventing new words and thinking about "wrong" ones, now consider words that make no sense at all, like **"kamraf."** Give it a meaning and describe how it's used, in the phrase "There's way too much kamraf around here!" or "What a sensational Kamraf."

*(Work in your notebook)*

Write a phrase with maximum **irony.** Something is ironic when it expresses a different or opposite meaning than that of a literal or intended initial meaning. Hard to explain, so here are some examples: A character screams about needing quiet, or thinks deeply about how shallow he is. An ironic event could be making a pantsuit out of your curtains, but being unable to try it on, since people can now easily look inside your room. What other ironic situations can you invent?

*(Work in your notebook)*

## LOADED WORDS

Certain words, loaded with meaning, make good writing triggers. Consider **"gravity",** the force of the earth as well as seriousness; **"birth"** of a creature, a concept or a trend; or **"home",** a plate to tag in baseball, the structure in which one lives or a deep feeling of security. **"Distant"** can mean far away geographically, or emotionally cool. Choose a word with multiple meanings, and pursue one or more of them, in a description or story. Be sure to fully describe your setting and the emotions of your characters.

*(Work in your notebook)*

**"String"** also leads to many ideas. A character might be tied up, strung along or at the end of his or her rope. Find some other words with various connections to string, then choose one aspect to **use in a story you illustrate**.

*(Work in your notebook)*

## BILINGUAL

Lots of people speak a few words in another language, and some speak two or more languages fluently. Sometimes, when you're speaking your native tongue, a word in a foreign language just crops up and expresses what you mean in a more forceful way:

*The surgeon went **LOCO** over the milkshake Roland made. She's the one who always dresses **TRES CHIC** under her scrubs.*

*Nestor's chandelier is **KAPUT**. You just had to juggle rocks, didn't you?*

*Wanda is the ultimate perfectionist, such an **ÜBERACHIEVER**!*

***MUY MACHO**, David pounded his chest, a true gorilla, and barged into lace making class.*

*(Work in your notebook)*

Write a story or a description using as many **foreign words** as you can. Who are your characters? What are their nationalities and where does your story take place? Are they fluent or trying to speak a second, third or fourth language? Are they understood or not? Misunderstandings can be unimportant, funny…or tragic. You decide!

If you're fluent in two languages, write a conversation between two characters that each only speak one language well. Find the words that help them communicate in **"Spanglish"**, **"Franglais"** or whatever their mixed languages would be.

*(Work in your notebook)*

Cathy wrote this poem in Franglais:

*C'est really très malin*

*To speak à mi-chemin*

*An odd verbal calin:*

*My rabbit parle lapin*

**"Since when do you have a rabbit?"**

**"It was just for the poem, Monsieur Jealous."**


Here's another one:

*Aux bons mots*

*Mon bon Momo*

*Flow l'encre du stylo*

*Aux pleurs des banjos*

*Et on with the show*

Your turn to **write a poem using two languages**:

*(Work in your notebook)*

## MAKING SENSE WHEN NOTHING DOES

Which languages don't you speak? Choose one, and write a poem, basing your words on sounds that seem possible. It's very creative to write in **a language you don't know**! This assignment was inspired by a concert of songs in Estonian, Swedish and Finnish. (If you put your poem to music, you're really have a great "song you don't know"!)

*(Work in your notebook)*

Write about **places that mix opposite notions**: The Alpine Desert, The Everglade Mountains, The Mohave Swamp, The Jungles of Norway, Mount Basin or Peak Valley. Don't be too literal, just invent what sort of place each might be.

*(Work in your notebook)*

What if the **ingredients in a recipe were fighting**? Would a sauce "subdue" a vegetable? Could a spice "enrage" a dairy product? Write your own "aggressive" recipe, describing the taste of the finished dish (unless it ends up on the wall!).

*(Work in your notebook)*

**Describe a place you've never been or an experience you've never had.** If you've never been in a luge race or walked on a tight rope, give describing what it would be like a shot. If you've never been in South America, try describing a small village there.

*(Work in your notebook)*

A word about **SUSPENSE**

*"Boo!"*

*"Too obvious, Nardo."*

Keeping a reader intrigued enough to keep turning pages takes originality. If your reader can predict your hero will make his way through cobwebs to open a closet and find a skeleton, you could use some fresh ideas. Better to have a juggler spring up and shout "Show time!"

Fill your writing with unexpected turns. And remember, no reader sticks with a story that's not gripping. First, you have to engage her interest, so she keeps reading even though she may be anxious about what's coming next.

Now, try writing a **suspenseful story**. How will you illustrate it? By drawing the scariest thing, or something not so scary? Either can work.

*(Write and draw in your notebook)*

As you work, remember to try **new things**, even if it makes you feel out of your element. If you usually write science fiction, try a love story that takes place in a simple, real setting. If you usually write about life by the sea, attempt an adventure in outer space. **Try a kind of story you've never written before.**

*(Work in your notebook)*

## EDITING

Time for the **editing experiment**! By now, you've generated lots of wonderful work. Choose a story or description you especially like, that needs some smoothing. Keep each draft as you proceed, so you won't hesitate to make daring choices.

Use a colored pencil to underline any things you think aren't essential in your original version. If you're on a computer, you can change the color of the type. Save this draft, then erase the words in color (or rewrite a new draft without them). Keep the next version, too.

Now read your shortened draft. Choose a different color to highlight any passage that needs more description or action. Remember two things: Your reader wants to follow a story that moves at a good pace and has probably read enough to not require too much explanation. Your goal should be to tell your story fully, in as few words as necessary. Choose just the right words, and "fully" and "few" won't seem contradictory.

Are you finding your latest draft better, crisper, with better "tension"? Good! Now, you're a real writer. "Writing is rewriting" goes the cliché. Can you invent a new saying about writing? Is it like throwing up the alphabet? Fishing for an idea in the stratosphere? Hearing a faraway melody and transcribing the notes as words?

*(Write your saying in your notebook)*

***It's not hard to attribute this quote: "Writing means capping your pen, then hiding in the cellar."***

There are always days when the words don't flow and a writer or artist feels stuck. Write about **"Artist's or Writer's Jail"**. What sort of place is it? What is prohibited? Are prisoners allowed to have pencils? Are they allowed to think? What are the smells and sounds of the place?

*(Work in your notebook)*

Remember your Fertile Factory, and write what creativity sounds like, feels like and smells like. Does it sound like pounding waves? Does it smell like brewing coffee? Does it feel like burlap to your fingertips? As with every exercise in this book, it's all up to you.

Are you tired of putting your brain to the test? Then try writing a story using **someone else's brain**. How could that work? How is the result different from a story you would write? Aha! Maybe you are writing it!

## CHAPTER SNAKE:

## RETURN OF THE BAD SEED

What happens next with Cathy and The Immortal Nard? Does she wrestle with him, then get fatally ill with peritonitis? Or is she miraculously saved? Does he become a better and more prolific writer and sign his numerous works with her name? Do they coexist peacefully forever, or do they forever struggle since she wants to be only the writer in her body? Does he leave her for another writer?

Figure it out, alone or with a group and send Cathy your ending to can.writing@gmail.com. Make sure to put "Nardo" in your subject line, so it won't go into a spam folder. The most creative ending will appear on Cathy's web site, promise.

Feel free to post a haiku and "like" Nardo's page on Facebook:
http://www.facebook.com/pages/Nardo-from-Write-Outside-the-Lines/277474782296350


To see what Cathy's up to
or arrange a workshop at your school, visit
http://can.writing.free.fr

# SPS*

# *Serpent's Post Scriptum

Well, how satisfying. You've finished the book and now you're as far outside the lines as I am. Personally, I hope you drop this interest in writing and pursue a worthwhile occupation, such as cloud counting or air mattress inflation.

Determined, are you? Oh, all right:

Picture attempting to write on a dreary day. You shiver in a threadbare, argyle sweater while an icy wind rattles your leaky windows. Barely a line has spilled onto the page. How you yearn for a jolt of hope, something that can create a seismic shift in your brain.

Enter, a virtual, caped cobra! Having benefitted from years of training with my writer host, the Immortal Nard has developed infallible guidelines and kept them hidden in a wall safe in Taravina. I present them for the first time now, for your relish and amazement:

Nardo's Negative Notions to beautify your brainwaves and glorify your guts.

## Take the Uncomfortable Path

Go straight to writing about what you don't want to write about. Take time intensive detours, and redefine words to describe them. Follow the direction that feels the most uncomfortable, since it will lead you to more original ideas. (Cathy will surely approve of the "original ideas part" but I'll wager this snaky supplement on "discomfort". Trust me.)

Oh, if only more writers considered things from the inner demons point of view! It's such a rich area, deep in the dark, dank core of a writer. You get to narrow your eyes at the world outside your innocuous host. It's a natural for turmoil. Do give it a whirl.

My fervent desire is that Cathy should exert herself and produce...Nothing. That beauteous void! The nil and null. The silence of doomed outer space. I devote my existence to extinguishing hers, I am that intense. But every good demon can find his or her own havoc to put on the agenda.

Now, allow your inner demon to list his or her goals.

Of course, sometimes it backfires. My lifelong devotion to diminishing Cathy's creative output often hurtles her into rebel territory, where she gets some of her best work done. So scuff your shoes, mess up your hair and untuck your shirt. Here we go.

Edgier emotions. There's a lot of energy in intense feelings: the desperate longing for a sip of water, unleashed fury at injustice, profound sadness at suffering. Take a stand and start to roar. It will all begin where your character becomes unhinged and can no longer respect the constraints of society. Forget manners and decorum and shoot for what's authentic.

Dire circumstances. What's more interesting, a character gazing out a window or teetering on the ledge? Extremes need not be dangerous, and you don't need to include wild actions that aren't related to your story. Just consider events that intensify your character's experiences and reactions.

Go out of bounds. Have your characters interact with people they'd never meet normally. People with strong feelings and unusual lives: lion tamers, inventors, gang members, politicians, intriguing foreigners.

Risks. Even if your character is prudent, have him take risks as never before. If he is a notorious risk taker, have him curtail his behavior and see how that feels. Fashion can be risky. What if a character changed himself entirely (appearance and behavior)? What might reveal the character's "true" image?

Defy destiny and oppose obvious reactions. Rejoice at bad weather.

MORE DESCRIPTIVE WRITING from the negative notebooks:

Describe a room your character hated occupying.

Describe the flow of images seen in a silent movie. Include the way characters move, the setting and scene transitions. No music allowed.

Describe a hiccup as poetically as possible, especially a hiccup that hurts.

Write a recipe for chaos. Be as outrageous or conservative as you like.

Cathy loves math. I dutifully reproduce for you here some of her Geometric writing models:

## Telescoping Stories

Step One: Choose any brief, unpleasant action and describe it in glorious detail.

Step Two: Now place that action within a larger story, and feel free to get as negative as you like.

The action may or may not be central to the story, but it should have a place nonetheless. For example, a character can prick his finger threading a needle, then drop it when the phone rings with a announcement of bad news. But you can take the story in any direction afterwards.

Or, you might focus on describing a character choosing a book to read from a list of dreadful options, then living the rest of his life like the dull, historical figure in the book...

You can also telescope down from a larger story to a smaller moment. A character might battle cold wind during a mountain climbing expedition, and pause one evening to miserably contemplate a leaf stuck to some mud on her boot.

Could the pause on its own become a short story? You may even bring about an upbeat ending or give things a positive twist, if you must...

Inspired by all the dancing we do around the apartment, here's the exercise Cathy calls Word Ballets

Write a scene as if it's a choreographed dance, describing the movement of an action as if it's being watched on stage. Consider ice cubes tumbling into a glass, the "dance" of waves on a shore or commuters getting off a train. What words will you choose to describe the quality of the movement? Haunting? Clunky? If it's "flowing or "graceful" maybe something dreadful could be included, for zip.

Scribbled on the back page of a notebook I found under some scarves in a drawer: Cathy's Creative Conundrums

Think how you might write a story with action and a setting, but no characters. Or, action and characters, but no setting. Or setting and characters, but no action.

Write a scene that takes place during a play, which is not in the play. It can be in the audience or backstage, or onstage, but not scripted.

Strange Situations from the Snake

A character finds a sizeable piece of raw meat on the street. Describe the unlikely way in which it got there. What are the consequences, if any?

Write about something going sideways. It could be a supermarket cart with wonky wheels or a rodeo horse.

Explore inertia. What can happen in your character's head as he stares at a wall, or stays in bed for 48 hours?

Write a scene or a story that involves any size or type of broken sink: metal, porcelain, plastic. In a prison, home, school, hospital, at a camp ground, on a boat...

Describe a dusty item bought in a resale shop, and the character that buys it. Would we have predicted that person would make that purchase?

Write a scene involving something that rolls. A coin, down the sewer? A head, on its way from the guillotine?

Dig up new characters (and be sure to wear sturdy gloves)

Go through a character's garbage to determine his or her identity.

Write about a character that hates a certain time of day. When and why? Find unusual examples, to make your character original.

Describe something a character keeps despite it being of no use to him/her. Has the character chosen to keep it, or is it kept unintentionally?

Write a scene in which a character brings a hand to his or her face at one point, with or without force. There are many ways and reasons for which this might happen.

Write about a character that's almost crushed in a crowd. Where and how?

Describe a character you don't know from the POV of a character you do know, or vice versa. You will define the character you don't know while completing this exercise.

A character buries an object as a war breaks out, then returns afterward and digs it up. Who did this, when and where was it done and what was buried?

Create a character that feels better when something bad happens to him (loses a wallet, misses a plane, breaks an arm). Explore even more unusual characters.

Write about a character that closes an eye or both eyes, for one reason or another.

## Presume identities

Who is the Tinker of Terror or the Zinc Zealot?

## Interrupt Thoughts

Eavesdrop on a conversation then let an original character spring to mind and enter the scene. Perhaps a window washer crashes in and disagrees with what was just said...

Or, take a conversation you've heard, and have it take a wild turn, writing something unrelated that leads the characters in a new direction.

You can also write the unspoken train of thought of one of the characters, what you imagine he or she could be thinking, while holding up one end of the conversation.

Break out some new phrases

Describe the sound of stained plaid. It may have nothing to do with Scottish bagpipes. Maybe it's a "ting" triangle contrasted with the rat tat tat of a jack hammer...

Write "The Banishment Song". What would the lyrics be? What is the tune?

Write a haiku about impatience, inventing words as you go.

Challenge dissenters. Who's "they", anyway?

Is there anyone who might have expectations about your writing? Here's a chance to make them powerless: write about them! Are they a panel of short, bald bespectacled judges who never make sense? Are they inanimate objects? Perhaps you're being judged by a toaster.

WRITE ABOUT A CHARACTER that can't make a move without considering what people think.

Write a poem about conformity (doing what everyone else is doing). When is being different a good idea? What might a character risk or gain?

Cathy would tell you to trust your instincts and not bother searching for "what readers want"; to write what you want and get your audience interested in that. She's also insist you come back to the book whenever you find yourself in a lull. (This "positive" kick she's on often makes me cringe, but it gives me an idea:

What happens when a character that gives pep talks needs a pep talk really badly? Write a few lines, and make your character desperate.)

Now, back to my lesson plan--- But, what is that infernal thumping noise? It seems to be coming from the crate where I managed to get Cathy, uh, resting...."What's that? Your voice is muffled. I can't hear you. What do you mean, 'More paper'? I gave you a whole page already. Besides,  I thought you were off giving a free workshop at a bookstore or teaching little children to sing 'The Itsy Bitsy Spider'. Okay, if you insist, you can have 'your' desk back...."

*Your writer doesn't mind taking a back seat for a chapter or two, as long as you're working on creative ideas, Nardo!*

*Readers, even after you go through all the exercises, you'll still be visited (and possibly restrained) from time to time by your creature within.*

*Here's a thought: What if a whole bunch of inner demons met for lunch one day? What would the conversation be? Who'd pay the bill? Would they leave the waiter a tip?*

*You'll need to respond to your demon with strength and determination each time. You know there are no wrong answers in creative writing. Now, go one step further and say that EVERY answer is right. All your ideas count, no matter how unpolished. Let them come find you and be sure to record them. You can always rework them later.* **Consider yourself an ever evolving, walking rough draft.**

*Another way to approach this:*

### *LISTEN TO THE HAND THAT DOESN'T WRITE*

*Remember the rational and intuitive sides of the brain? There's a lot of symmetry and opposition in human beings. Most of us write with one hand, but we have two. The hand that writes knows about good penmanship, that a verb is an action word and where the commas go. Cathy thinks of the other hand as an intuitive one, to balance the practicality of the writing hand.*

*For all your creative work,* **listen regularly to the hand that doesn't write***. It feels without following any rules. This intuitive hand is an important part of you. Let it help you get hold of your creative ideas.*

**Write down a few ideas you get from your hand that doesn't write.**

*Now, try an exercise letting your intuitive side lead:*

**Confetti** *is found in the pocket of a coat a character hasn't worn for some time. What has changed since the day the confetti got there?*

*One of the benefits from this approach is, while Nardo can nip the hand that writes, he barely notices the other hand, so never condemns its creative contributions!*

Oh yeah? Get a load of these parting words: Beware all ambidextrous amphibians!

*Did you really think Cathy would give Nardo the last WORD? --- Whisper your answer, so he doesn't hear. He just put his headphones on to enjoy some atonal futuristic for bongos and harpsichord, so this will have to be quick....*

*Cathy enjoys letting the dear snake assume some teaching responsibilities. It's good for his confidence, which has been so very shaky of late. What difference could it make if Cathy or Nardo teaches; you know all these pages come from the same brain, anyway, right? To be honest, at times, it's hard to be sure....Especially when Nardo so vividly describes his recurrent dreams about the mongoose. She's sort of a demon's demon. It only makes sense inner demons would have demons, too. Hey! Consider the possibilities of that idea:*

### Write about your demon's demon

*(Work in your notebook)*

*Nardo's mongoose is significantly larger than he is, for maximal intimidation. And three guesses what he calls her: CATHY!! Do you think she should take this as a compliment?*

*In any case, it's now time for certain authors to go to sleep. As she dims the lights, allow Cathy to wish you all a magnificent future of thinking and writing.*

*And do stay tuned for more adventures with Cathy, Nardo and the Mongoose.*

*Must you refer to me as 'The Mongoose'? I happen to have a name: Sloopy, and I just printed out a draft of my memoir, in case you're interested: (throat clearing noise) 'Life began in a sunny yet festering-----'*

How tragic, readers! Cathy's printer must be out of ink. Her fault, entirely. I only managed to write these last lines because I came upon a spare cartridge while rifling her drawers looking for postage stamps. Big news: I'm about to send away for a mongoose muzzle! So much to do, so little time... Do keep yourselves amused, won't you?

NARDO

*It really never stops, does it?*

*WORD!*

*Cathy*

## Acknowledgements

My gratitude to Jill Neimark for getting me thinking about creative thinking, to Betty Heller for her thoughtful comments on the manuscript and to Andrea Renner Ipaktchi, for her delightfully creative input. Thanks to Manny Mendelson and Bill Stamets for their help proofreading. I am grateful to my husband, Pascal, for bringing Nardo to life, to Arlene Wanetick, for her heartfelt encouragement, and to Ben Voyles, for his pertinent insights and scathing humor. Deepest thanks to Helen Sahin Connelly of Gifted in France, for opening so many doors, and to Cybèle Troyan, my wonderful artist partner for workshops and camps. And, unending gratitude to Lynne Patchett Field, for her suggestion that started it all, in 2008, "Why don't you teach a writing class?" It changed my life.

**Educators and parents write about WOTL:**

"What happens when you put Robin Hood in the sewer with a band of merry microbes? Or start a story on the inside of an eyeball? You discover the wonderful, outlaw joy of writing a story that no one else has dared try before. In "Write Outside the Lines" Cathy Altman Nocquet shows aspiring writers of any age how to have more fun -- and be more productive -- than they ever thought possible.

For anyone who has laughed at a Neil Gaiman story, shivered at the plot twists of J.K. Rowling or gasped at one of Michael Chabon's concoctions -- and then wondered: "Why can't we teach anything like that in school?" -- the answer is: "Now we can." WOTL is the most ingenious, subversive, life-affirming textbook that I've ever encountered. It's a book that will inspire a new generation of great writers, and help even the most apprehensive students discover that, yes, writing can be wonderful."
  *George Anders, New York Times best-selling author and co-recipient of the Pulitzer Prize for national reporting, 1997.*

"In an inspiring and instructive book that captures the essence of her unique creative writing classes, Cathy Altman Nocquet frees readers of all ages to write with confidence and courage."
  *Sheila Kohler, O'Henry Prize winning author and  Lecturer, Princeton University*

"As modern learning and brain science show, it takes a village to raise a creative child and Cathy shows how to create this village one story at a time."
  *Charles Vanover, PhD, Professor of Education, USF*

"'The 'go to' handbook for creative writing classes at all levels, WOTL contains a mind-boggling array of exercises, that are, in themselves, an extraordinary display of creativity."
  *Mendelson Research Chicago*

"Most books that teach writing lead the neophyte to shut down instead of open up. WOTL shows us the only way to find your "voice" as a writer: by taking ownership of that thing you've been hiding inside all these years, stripping it naked and letting it howl at the moon"
*Ernie the Writing Guru*

"A witty book composed of outrageous, succinct thought experiments…. Making a central character of that inner voice that prevents us from following our dreams is a brilliant about face."
*Margaret Olin, PhD,*
*Senior Research Scholar Yale University*

"Open this book and creativity will seep into your daily life. You'll feel mentally limber, and always leave your notepad with a sense of serenity. Cathy's exercises are like yoga for the right brain; the book should come with creative writing attire."
*Andi Ipaktchi, Visual Artist*

"Thank you for making me write. First time in ages."
*Penelope Fletcher, Owner, Red Wheelbarrow Bookstore*

**Educators and parents write about the workshops:**

"I have never seen nor heard of anyone who works with people, young and old, in as inspiring a way as Cathy Altman Nocquet in her creative writing workshops. With cunning wit and depth of understanding, she opens her students' minds to the endless possibilities of their own imaginations, giving them the skills and direction to put this into words, sounds, rhythms and phrases."

*Amy Gamlen, Musician and Composer, Paris Jazz
Underground, April 2010*

"Cathy has a magic that seems effortless: she is able to inspire confidence, imagination, and devoted writing in her students. When we co-teach workshops with the goal of staging original stories, written collaboratively by the participants, the staging AND the writing complement each other perfectly. All of this springs from Cathy's charismatic style. She is in creative complicity with each of her students, and the results are joyful to behold."

*Susan Harloe, Artistic Director, Word for Word
Performing Arts Company, San Francisco*

"As parents, we are always delighted and touched to read the results of creative sessions with you."

*M.S. June, 2010*

"Your assignments for the kids sure beat 500 words on the history of diesel power plants in Tanzania. I want to transfer out of my section."

*B.V. June, 2010*

"I love taking adventures down the wild paths of your mind. Thanks for the voyage."

*J.B. June, 2010*

"You are like the Grand Rabbi of Minsk where all of the peoples of Eastern Europe bask in your sagacious wisdom."

*Scott S. May, 2010*

## IDEAS

Made in the USA
Columbia, SC
23 March 2018